A GODLY
LIFE
Companion

A True Testimony Of Life
With A Woman Of Destiny

CELESTIN MUTABARUKA

*"He who finds a wife finds a good thing
and obtain favour from the Lord."*
—Proverbs 18:22.

*"An excellent wife, who can find?
For her worth is far above jewels!"*
—Proverbs 31:10.

*"House and wealth are an inheritance from fathers,
but a prudent wife is from the Lord."*
— Proverbs 19:14.

GOD, MY HEAVENLY FATHER:

That time I went on my knees, I said a prayer;
You heard my prayer and answered me;
You gave me the right one.
Thank you so much!

TABLE OF CONTENTS

ENDORSEMENTS

What a book! Faith building, ministerial and spiritual lessons, apart from exemplary family living. Truly, this is the experiential display of Proverbs 31.

I strongly recommend that this is a must read book to all ministers of the gospel, full time and part time, lay leaders and even ordinary church members of all cultural backgrounds.

Yes, this book is about an astounding power of God beginning in the life of one woman, Rose, engulfing one man, Celestin and being imparted to five prophetic children. However, may I also pen it down here by the grace of God upon me that the future of this family is of an unveiling power of God, and a testimony that will by far exceed anything narrated herein.

Rev. Dr. George Kenan Nywage, MATh, ThD
Overseer, KLPT Tanga Provinve, Tanzania
Principal, Tanga Christian Bible College, Tanga, Tanzania.

In the book of Revelation 12:10-11 we read:
"And I heard a loud voice saying in heaven, Now is come salvation, and strength, and the kingdom of our God, and the power of his Christ: for the accuser of our brethren is cast down, which accused them before our God day and night. And they overcame him by the blood of the Lamb, and by the word of their testimony; and they loved not their lives unto the death" (KJV).

In *A Godly Life Companion: A True Testimony Of Life With A Woman Of Destiny*, just like any other book, readers are destined to see different things depending on their orientation and gratification. But as the sub tittle reveals, this book is a testimony, and that promptly makes it a *weapon*. A weapon because, as we have just seen in the above quotation, testimony is one of the weapons by which we overcome the accuser of brethren.

Since the enemy was cast down on earth, life has been a continuous battle of one kind or the other. In this book, the reader will see how a life of commitment and sacrifice (not loving life unto death) generated testimonies that not only brought victory for pastor Mutabaruka and his family but also people they have come into contact with through the years.

The author introduces his wife as a woman of destiny. He then proceeds to demonstrate this by showing how from childhood, Rose' life was divinely channelled so that at every point and turn there unfolded God's purposes—purposes that were impossible to estimate at the initial stages. For example, Pastor Mutabaruka tells of a decision Rose made when she was faced with options that couldn't have been difficult for most of us. The decision she made deserved to be described as 'foolish.' Rose had been admitted to pursue a dream degree course in arguably the most prestigious university in East Africa at the time. Convinced that God had spoken to her against taking up her place at the university, it was a mark of a rare obedience that she settled for a diploma course in forestry from a college located in a remote place in Tanzania. I highlight this story because for me, it became an emotional point of her story because it was through this 'foolish' detouring that she finally found her way into Kenya where the Lord Jesus used her to lead me to salvation in a spectacular way—a way that I feel only Rose could do.

I highly recommend *A Godly Life Companion: A True Testimony Of Life With A Woman Of Destiny*. In this book, don't expect to read a subjective praise of a husband for a wife, rather, like the Acts of the Apostles, expect to read chronicles of the workings of the Holy Spirit in the life of a woman of destiny. The story will enrich your soul especially when you recognise the impact of the interplay between God's leading and the servant's obedience.

Be blessed as you read.

Pastor Daniel O. Ogweno
Author: The Pursuit of Commitment.

ABOUT THE AUTHOR

Celestin Mutabaruka holds a BSc Degree in Forestry and M.Phil. in Forest Economics (both from Moi University, Eldoret, Kenya). He also holds PhD in Agricultural Sciences (Imperial College London, University of London).

He is married to Dr. Rose Mutabaruka, the one whose accolade is the subject of this book.

Rose and Celestin are blessed with five children: Three daughters: Blandina-Gratia, Gloria-Damaris, Deborah-Princess and two sons: Peter-Shalom and Isaiah-Prince.

CHAPTER 1

INTRODUCTION

ROSE: A plant that typically bears and adorns red, pink, yellow, or white fragrant flowers. Rose is a beauty known not only for her exceptional elegance and special fragrance, but also for her enduring symbol of love.

The One This Book is About

This book is about Rose, my wife and the mother to our precious sons and daughters. It contains life experiences out of which I have collected testimonies. Over the years, speaking and reminiscing with Rose, her family and friends that she grew up and schooled with, has given me something to write about and share with others.

Words are not enough to express my gratitude to God for giving me His daughter as a life companion. I have enjoyed living with this anointed woman of God and can openly confess that I have always been satisfied by her company along this long journey on earth. I give all the glory and honour to God.

During my times of joy, she is always the first to rejoice and celebrate with me. Whenever I pass through the valleys of tough circumstances and tribulations, when friends and confidants have scurried a mile from me, she has always remained next to me, whispering to my ear that she would never leave me nor forsake me even if it means dying with me.

This woman has learnt to endure my imperfections and has been key in my progression in faith in the Lord, always devising wise ways so that I may move to the next level. She told me that God spoke to her and said that He has given her an assignment to help me at any cost along the journey to heaven. Her obedience to that divine instruction has rather been clear to me through many circumstances that we have passed through as a family.

> Words are not enough to express my gratitude to God for giving me His daughter as a life companion.

Rose's love for the Lord is resolute; her resolve evident, and her evidence tangible. That love has never lessened but has grown to higher dimensions; discovering new horizons of intimacy with God; spurred by an adventurous faith; exploring the divine dimensions; seeking the kingdom of God with enthusiasm and unrelenting commitment. She is a peculiar woman of God, a Nazirite.

Rose's Childhood

Rose, the last born among seven siblings, was born on 1st February 1959 in Itandula, a small village in the Njombe District of the United Republic of Tanzania, formerly known as Tanganyika. Her father, Timoth Mangula and mother, Blandina Tulamuwona Ng'amilo, were Christians and committed servants of God in the Lutheran Church of Tanganyika. My father-in-law was an evangelist who was always busy preaching the Gospel of the Lord Jesus Christ in his community.

In most circumstances, behind an active and anointed man of God, is a holy woman of God who does not necessarily conduct great public crusades like the husband, but who tremendously contributes to the success of her husband's ministry by just being on her knees, interceding. Rose' mother was such a woman. She was a committed believer who was unreservedly supporting her husband's ministry in addition to raising their two sons and five daughters.

God performed great signs and wonders in the ministry of Timoth Mangula. As this book is about Rose and not her father, I shall not go into details about how God used Evangelist Timoth Mangula and his ministry, hoping that if the Lord tarries, Rose and I shall have another opportunity to compile a different testimony about her dad's ministry in a different book. Those signs and wonders are thrilling. Please pray for the success of this project as the testimony will certainly edify the Body of Christ.

CHAPTER 2

WALKING WITH GOD SINCE CHILDHOOD

*"I am reminded of your sincere faith, which first
lived in your grandmother Lois and in your mother
Eunice and, I am persuaded, now lives in you also"
(2 Timothy 1:5).*

God's Provision Using the Hand of a Child

*J*anet is the first born in the Mangula's family. After she had been away in her matrimonial home for many years, she went back to Itandula village to visit her parents, siblings and relatives. She went with her four children. During those days there were no efficient means of communication in Tanzania, therefore, she didn't communicate to her parents that she was due to visit them. Nevertheless, the unexpected visit was such a sweet surprise for Timoth and his wife. They were extremely happy to see their first born after many years.

In African culture, when you get an important visitor, you butcher either a cow, a sheep, a goat or a cock depending on what is available and the regard accorded to the said visitor. A visitor causes people to celebrate. The fact that Janet had come along with four children that her parents had not seen before made the occasion even more special. Unfortunately, there was no animal to slaughter. My father-in-law therefore ambled around, working out a plan how to get his hands on an animal so as to make the occasion special for his daughter, grandchildren and the family.

Meanwhile, Rose was sent to draw water from the nearby well. Contrary to the comfort enjoyed by people in the developed world, many homes in rural Africa do not have tap water. People have to get water from wells, rivers or lakes.

On her way back, Rose heard what she felt was someone or something sprinting at high speed in the nearby savannah. She heard the thing fall a few feet away from where she was. Curious about what it could have been, she placed her water container down; turned and walked to check what it was. She was surprised to find that it was an animal they call "swala" (an antelope) lying there. This animal was in high demand for its delicious meat. The locals used to hunt it and sell its meat in that area for a dear price.

As the animal was lying on the ground, Rose took a wooden stick and hit the animal several times on the neck until the animal was completely weakened, it was still alive though. Since the animal was big (bigger than the size of an adult goat or sheep), Rose could not carry it home, so she left it on the site and rushed home to report the event to her father. At first, the father didn't believe her because it normally takes experienced hunters to get the *swala*, but due to Rose' insistence, the father decided to go with her to the site, not expecting to see the animal, but to stop her from nagging him.

When they arrived, the animal was still there struggling to stand on its feet but without success as it had been immobilized by Rose. My father-in-law was absolutely amazed. He took the animal home, slaughtered it and then prepared it. There was plenty of meat for the whole family and he was even able to give some to the neighbours. Everyone was so surprised how this child discovered the animal and had courage to weaken it rather than running away from it because of fear, as many children, especially girls, would do. What happened was a divine provision and God used the hand of a child to bless the whole family.

> On her way back, Rose heard what she felt was someone or something sprinting at high speed in the nearby savannah. She heard the thing fall a few feet away from where she was.

God knows and cares about every single detail of our life, glory be to His Holy Name! God was concerned that His faithful servant had no goat or sheep to slaughter for the celebration of his daughter's and grand-children's special visit. Jehovah Jireh indeed provided miraculously. This reminds me of what happened on Mount Moriah when Abraham had no sheep to sacrifice and miraculously the Lord provided a lamb.

> But the angel of the Lord called out to him from heaven, "Abraham! Abraham!"
> "Here I am," he replied.
> "Do not lay a hand on the boy," he said. "Do not do anything to him. Now I know that you fear God, because you have not withheld from me your son, your only son." Abraham looked up and there in a thicket he saw a ram caught by its horns. He went over and took the ram and sacrificed it as a burnt offering instead of his son. So Abraham called that place The Lord Will Provide. And to this day it is said, "On the mountain of the Lord it will be provided.—Genesis 22:11-14.

Hearing the Voice of God

"Uncle is not dead!"

From tender age, it was evident that God had chosen to speak to Rose in supernatural ways. The following story Rose told me explains this.

Her uncle, Martin Mangula, the elder and only living brother to her father, was at their house, visiting. One day, Rose and her dad left the uncle at home with other relatives. Her dad was to conduct a funeral ceremony somewhere not very far from their village. Towards the end of the burial event, a messenger came from their home running, gasping and wailing inconsolably. He reported that Rose's uncle, Martin, had died suddenly.

The messenger was a grown up person who, together with other neighbours, had tried to help Rose' uncle in his last hour. There was not much they could do to revive him, he finally breathed his last.

They wrapped the body in a blanket according to the way it was done in their customs and laid it on a bed. The people present there knew beyond any reasonable doubt that he was truly dead. That is why they dispatched the messenger to go and break the sad news to Rose' father.

When Rose' father heard about it, he almost collapsed—strength was completely drained from him. People around him at the time had to hold him by the arms in order to give him support.

When Rose saw her dad in that helpless situation, she went forward and told him and the people who were comforting him not to worry because her uncle had not died. Nobody including her father was willing to listen to her since she was a young girl of about 11years old. They were sure that Rose didn't know what she was taking about. How did she know that her uncle was not actually dead?

"I heard something telling me in my heart that my uncle was not dead and then I decided to tell them", says Rose.

As expected, Rose' father cut short his appointment where he had gone to conduct a funeral ceremony. He headed home, accompanied by a good number of comforters. Rose also followed them but she didn't keep the pace. The procession to their home was that of sorrow and wailing. They all pitied Rose' father as this was his only brother left and one whom he loved dearly. It was such a big matter for him to lose his only remaining brother.

As they headed home, everybody was bawling except Rose. She wasn't emotionally overwhelmed by sorrow like the rest because she had heard a voice assuring her that her uncle was not dead.

Some people rushed ahead hastily, reaching before the rest of the party. When they entered the room where the body was laid, they were astonished to find Rose' uncle seated on the bed with his back to the wall, smiling. As expected, everyone was dumbfounded. They stood there for what felt like forever, not sure whether they were dreaming or it was indeed a reality. Shortly after, Rose' dad also arrived with the others that had been left behind. When they entered the house, Rose' father, sobbing and anxious to see the body of his brother, found himself like others, standing still as he saw his brother sitting up on the bed, very much alive. The wailing had stopped suddenly but it was replaced by bewilderment.

In this state of awe, one of them remembered that Rose had told them that her uncle was not dead. They all wondered how she had known about it. Rose didn't keep the pace and this was partly because she lacked the urge to hurry home, and also because she got distracted by a sugarcane she was chewing. Somebody had to be sent for her. She was told that her uncle was not dead after all.

"I told them but they didn't believe me!" Rose responded.

Everyone was interested to know how she knew that her uncle was not dead. She explained to them: "Something told me in my heart that my uncle was not dead and I told you but nobody took me seriously."

Everyone was amazed and gave thanks to God. The environment of mourning suddenly changed into an environment of joy and praise to God—it was a time of laughter and great celebration. They had witnessed two miracles: A man coming back to life and a small girl knowing about it beforehand.

Rose didn't keep the pace and this was partly
because she lacked the urge to hurry home, and also

because she got distracted by a sugarcane she was chewing.

Just as God started talking to Samuel from his very young age, Rose also started to enjoy the same fellowship from the time she was a child before she even started primary school. The revelation she received concerning her uncle was one of her early experiences of hearing the voice of God. As Samuel was not able to discern God's voice at the beginning, I believe that this was also the case with Rose. It is why when asked how she knew that the uncle was not dead, she answered that "something" had told her. That *something* was God speaking to her.

> Then the Lord called Samuel. Samuel answered, "Here I am." And he ran to Eli and said, "Here I am; you called me." But Eli said, "I did not call; go back and lie down." So he went and lay down.
> Again the Lord called, "Samuel!" And Samuel got up and went to Eli and said, "Here I am; you called me." "My son," Eli said, "I did not call; go back and lie down." Now Samuel did not yet know the Lord: The word of the Lord had not yet been revealed to him. A third time the Lord called, "Samuel!" And Samuel got up and went to Eli and said, "Here I am; you called me." Then Eli realized that the Lord was calling the boy. So Eli told Samuel, "Go and lie down, and if he calls you, say, 'Speak, Lord, for your servant is listening.'" So Samuel went and lay down in his place. The Lord came and stood there, calling as at the other times, "Samuel! Samuel!" Then Samuel said, "Speak, for your servant is listening." And the Lord said to Samuel: "See, I am about to do something in Israel...—1 Samuel 3:4-11.

The lost watch

On another occasion, my father-in-law lost his watch in the bush. For many hours, Rose' sisters and brothers together with their dad searched for it but without success. In the evening, as it was getting dark, they decided to stop the search and went back home. When they arrived home, a voice spoke to Rose and instructed her to go and search her father's watch.

She was assured that she would find the lost watch on condition that she followed the voice's instruction. She then swiftly left the house, followed the guidance of that voice, and finally arrived at the place where the watch was. She took it to her father. In amazement, the father wondered how Rose knew where the watch was. When she narrated how the voice led her to the location where the watch was, everyone was amazed. Her father was very pleased to have his watch back. He glorified God for the miracle. He marvelled how God is using his youngest daughter. The voice that was speaking and guiding Rose was the Holy Spirit.

Time of Great Shock

My mother-in-law passed away when Rose was still a young girl in primary school. It was such a painful experience for the whole family and to Rose especially as the last born still at tender age. She was still heavily reliant upon the love, affection and guidance of a mother. She still needed her in every way to guide her as she grew into a young lady. Despite these difficult moments, Rose experienced an overwhelming sense of God's love and the covering of His grace. She believes that she was firmly embraced by the heavenly Father who comforted her and took away sorrow far from her.

Rose remembers very well that while everyone else in the family was crying because of the sudden departure of their mother, she was the only one who was not crying. In fact, concerned about the impression her composure could portray, she went to the extent of faking grief. How could she fail to cry yet she had lost a mother—didn't she love her mother? In order to feign grief and wear a mourning mood, she rubbed spit on her eyes and cheeks to give the impression to her siblings that she was also crying. Deep in her heart however, she was not grieving like the rest. Although she was still young, at the age of eleven years she was old enough to understand the weight of the loss

26

that visited their family. It was God who did something spectacular to protect her from grief.

During the days that followed the death of her mother, Rose' father together with her brothers and sisters tried their best to surround Rose with love and affection, worried that perhaps the loss would sink in and hit her hard at a later stage. However, God's grace was abundant enough to outlast the grieving period and beyond.

Rose is forever thankful to God for that gracious comfort He surrounds her with, and also to her father and siblings for love and affection.

CHAPTER 3

AMAZING CONVERSION AND PARTAKING OF CHRIST'S SUFFERINGS

Hide your faith in Christ in your heart. Even if they were to beat and break your body, you shouldn't allow them to break into your heart and steal your faith. Guard your heart therefore with all zeal.

Amazing Conversion

*A*fter her primary education at Wanging'ombe School, Rose was among the only three students who satisfied the requirements of the National Examinations for that year to qualify for a government secondary school.

During those days, the competition was so stiff that a very limited number of pupils (less than 5% of year 6 pupils countrywide) were selected to join government secondary schools. The selection criterion was based on the students' academic performance. This is different from what happens in the developed world where access to government secondary schools is guaranteed to every primary school pupil regardless of his/her academic performance.

Rose joined a Girls' Secondary School for her Ordinary (O) Level education. It was one of the most prestigious government schools in the Province of Iringa. Although it was a government school, it was managed by catholic nuns and co-sponsored by the Catholic Church.

One evening, the nuns in charge of the school invited a team of people to come and show a Christian film to students about the life of Jesus Christ. All students and teachers settled in their seats in the school auditorium. While the team was setting up the film, one member of the team, a man from the Democratic Republic of Congo (then Zaïre), took his guitar and 'entertained' the audience, but as it turned out, it was something more than just an entertainment. He sang a Kiswahili song as follows:

Kama bahari ina mawimbi mengi,
Ukiwa na shaka na hofu,
Ikiwa huna budi kuacha ng'ambo,
na kutii Neno la Mungu.
Kipeleke chombo mbali na pwanilo,
kilindini umngojee Yesu,
Mle ufuoni mwa Genezareti
Utaona shabaha yake.

The English translation of the song is the following:

When the waves in the sea are raging;
When you have doubt and fear;
You have no choice but to leave the other side,
And obey the Word of God.
Take your vessel away from the shore
There in the deep sea, wait for Jesus,
There in the sea of Genezareth
You will see His purpose for you.

After this song, the Congolese man gave a short testimony about the saving power of the Lord Jesus and the beauty of salvation. While giving this testimony, the headmistress became upset and immediately interrupted him and commanded him to stop any form of preaching. "You have been requested to show the film and not to preach to students," she ordered. The man apologized and few minutes later, the film started.

The words of the song that the man sang however sank deep in Rose' heart. A void was created in her heart. Tears started flowing from her eyes, weeping unexplainably. She did not even concentrate watching the film, instead, she continued to meditate upon the words of the song and the singer's short interrupted testimony concerning the way he received the Lord Jesus Christ as his personal Saviour.

After the film, all the students went back to their dormitories to sleep. The whole night, Rose couldn't sleep as tears continuously rolled down her cheeks. She meditated on the love of Jesus and pondering the words of the testimony of the Congolese man. At the same time, the void in her heart continued to increase remarkably. She felt the urge and the immediacy in her heart to give her life to the Lord Jesus Christ. She, however, had no clue how to go about it. She spent the whole night wondering about how she could be saved.

The following morning, she woke up early while everyone else was still in bed. She was up early to meet her closest friend Rosemary. Rosemary used to sleep in a different dormitory. Rose wanted to share with her friend about her experience from the time the Congolese man sung at the auditorium and the impact of the words of his testimony. She also wanted to tell her friend how she spent a sleepless night shedding tears, wondering about how to get saved.

Whilst on the way to her friend's room, they bumped into each other in the corridor joining the two dorms. Astonishingly, Rosemary was also heading towards Roses' room to tell her about what had happened to her that night. It was pretty the same story. She had also spent a sleepless night shedding tears, feeling an immense emptiness in her heart following the song, testimony and film from that evening. What a coincidence!

Rosemary expected to get a satisfactory explanation of what was taking place in her heart from her friend because Rose was the chairlady of the Protestant Christian Union in the school. Rosemary was however disappointed because her friend, despite being the chairlady of the Christian Union, also had no idea about how to get saved as she too was not born again.

Rose was a good girl raised up in a Christian home but she had not come to a personal encounter with the Lord Jesus Christ. In other words, she had not officially acknowledged Jesus as her personal Saviour. She was a good religious girl but had nothing spiritual to offer to her friend.

The two girls and their other two friends decided to ask for permission to go to Iringa town to inquire from all churches the whereabouts of the ministering team that was at their school the previous night. As Rose' conduct in school was very good and well known by the school management, the nuns who were leading the school were neither suspicious nor worried about any involvement of those girls with bad company in town. As long as Rose was with them, there was no cause of alarm. The permission was granted and the four girls set off.

In those days, Good News of salvation was not preached in some popular well established churches. Their search was therefore targeting evangelical churches. On the way, the girls met a man and asked him whether he could be aware of any church in town which tells people to get saved. The man laughed and told them that there was one in town but in order to become a member, one important condition must be fulfilled. The girls asked the man what the condition was. The man said that the only condition was to cry and fill one cup with tears as everyone in that church cries during prayers. He gave them the direction to reach the church. Rose and Rosemary said to each other that the condition of filling a cup with tears was a simple one taking into consideration the amount of tears they shed the previous night. According to them, their tears could fill many cups. The girls were very excited to know the place and the direction to reach there. They went ahead with their journey.

On their arrival at that church, they found the people they wanted to meet praying together with other believers. These people were so excited and full of joy when they saw the girls knocking at the door. They welcomed them with love and told them that they were indeed waiting for them. Obviously, the girls were surprised to hear that they were expected while they had no pre-arranged appointment with them. How did they know that the four girls were coming?

In their prayers, God had revealed to the group that some girls from Iringa Girls would come to be saved, that is why they were eagerly expecting to see them, and when the girls showed up, their hearts were filled with joy, amazed at God's precision in everything He says and does. This was amazing!

The reader who does not know or believe that God speaks to His children and reveals many issues to them before they happen, will bear with me. Nevertheless, as my reader develops interest in the knowledge of God and hungers for intimacy with Him, he/she will find himself/ herself living this truth almost on a daily basis.

The girls were warmly welcomed and asked the purpose of their visit even though the brethren were already aware of it through the divine revelation. This can be likened to Christ who, on a number of occasions, asked people what they wanted Him to do for them even though He (Jesus) already knew what they wanted (Mark 10:46-51, John 5:6). It was like Christ saying: *I know what you want but you still have to ask for it* (Matt. 6:8).

The man said that the only condition was to cry and fill one cup with tears as everyone in that church cries during prayers.

The girls introduced themselves to their hosts and then went straight to the subject matter for their visit. They told their hosts that they wanted to know more about salvation following the song that was sung by the Congolese man, his testimony and the film that was shown in their school the night before.

Basic but fundamental facts about salvation through the accomplished redemptive work at Calvary by the Saviour Jesus Christ was clearly explained to the girls. They were then asked if they were willing to welcome the Lord Jesus in their lives as their personal Saviour. The question must have been rhetorical to them. To get saved was the reason they were there. All the four of them received Jesus in their lives—they got saved. They were led into the sinner's prayer of repentance. This was an important beginning of a new chapter in the girls' lives.

Contrary to what they were told by the man they had asked about a church where they could be saved, there was nothing about crying and filling a cup with tears.

Rose testifies that a heavy burden was lifted off her shoulders; her heart filled with exceptional joy and her mouth filled with laughter and praises to God. The sweet and powerful presence of God was real in the room to the point that the girls did not want to go back to school. They wanted to remain in that divine atmosphere in the presence of God, but the brethren urged them to go back to school before it was late. They reluctantly went back, but filled with thanksgiving to God for saving them.

Rose' First Sermon Ever

When the girls returned to school, they did not understand how the news reached their comrades that they had gone out to town to get saved. Many curious students rushed towards them to see how the saved people look like, whether their physical appearance had changed or not. As hundreds of students gathered around them, the bell rang calling all students to go into the dining room for their supper. Due to the joy of salvation, Rose had no appetite and did not want to eat anything that evening. She says that the joy of salvation that she had received that day was enough. She remained standing in the corridor meditating on the goodness of the Lord.

As she was standing in the corridor, something absolutely wonderful happened to her. Supernatural joy filled her heart to the point that she suddenly started speaking in unknown language. Rose says that she has never experienced such a great joy again. While speaking in tongues, she asked herself what kind of language was it she was speaking. A strange thought was injected in her mind (obviously from Satan) that probably she was becoming crazy but she said to herself that if getting crazy brings such great joy, then it is nice to be crazy. She says that the joy she had was unique.

Rose was not getting crazy but rather overflowing with the Spirit of God. She had received the baptism in the Holy Spirit. That day was a day of a triple portion of blessing:

i) She received Jesus Christ as her personal Saviour;

ii) Was baptized in the Holy Spirit, and

iii) Received the gift of speaking in tongues.

When she received the baptism in the Holy Spirit in the corridor, all students were still in the dining hall.

After this marvelous experience, Rose heard a voice instructing her to go into one of the classrooms. She obeyed and went in. There was nobody in the classroom, only chairs. The same voice that spoke to her said: *Open your Bible and read Romans 10:9-10* where it is written:

> If you declare with your mouth, "Jesus is Lord," and believe in your heart that God raised him from the dead, you will be saved. For it is with your heart that you believe and are justified, and it is with your mouth that you profess your faith and are saved.

She was then instructed by the same voice to read that scripture loudly and start preaching and witnessing to those chairs using the same scripture. This sounded crazy from the human point of view, but she chose to obey the sweet voice she had heard. Under heavy anointing, she started preaching to those chairs, witnessing to them about the love of Jesus and His saving power. This preaching took 3 to 5 minutes. After this, the same voice that told her to go into that classroom instructed her to go out therefrom and stand in the corridor where she was before. She obeyed, left the classroom and stood in the corridor.

Many curious students rushed towards them to see how the saved people look like, whether their physical appearance had changed or not.

Within a short while, students came out of the dining room and every one of them was rushing to meet Rose once again. The whole school assembled around her. The voice that spoke earlier to Rose spoke again, saying:

Now start preaching to the people surrounding you the same message you preached to chairs.

She obliged and immediately started witnessing to hundreds of students. The presence of God overwhelmed the place and the Spirit of God set upon His work in the hearts of the students.

As on the day of Pentecost when people of Jerusalem asked Peter what they should do to get saved (Acts 2:37), the same question was asked by hundreds of crying students. The girls asked Rose what they should do to receive the Lord Jesus Christ as their personal Saviour. Rose led them into the sinner's prayer of repentance and reconciliation with God through Jesus Christ. She did exactly as the brethren who prayed for her and her friends did at the church in Iringa town. Many students accepted the Lord Jesus Christ as their Saviour and welcomed Him in their hearts. That evening, there was great joy and jubilation in the whole school. As expected, this great revival didn't take long before it attracted the attention of the school administration.

Partaking of Christ's Sufferings Began in Earnest

There is a price to pay! The devil would not sit back and watch the girls excel in their salvation without moving in to nip the new life at the bud. Receiving salvation is free, but keeping it can be costly. This was the grim reality the girls soon came to confront. For those who have tasted the true grace of salvation and are committed to the hope of glory, there is no price intimidating enough to shy from.

The news reached the school administration that something strange had happened to students because of Rose; that an unknown cult had been introduced in the school. The following day, all students were assembled and told to stop the religious "nonsense" with immediate effect and, specifically, forget about salvation. The students already on fire for God were rather jubilating, thanking Him for His goodness and mercies. Those who received Jesus as Saviour were not ready to renounce Him. Rose was then summoned and rebuked for disseminating what they called "confusion" among students.

In some African countries, a whip is still used in schools to discipline students in primary and lower secondary levels. Rose was given a harsh punishment of that nature. She was whipped by the school leaders who vowed to continue with the same punishment until salvation was wiped out of her. After administering that punishment, they would ask whether salvation had gone out of her completely or not. The poor girl, shedding tears from the beating, replied, "It is very difficult to take it out of me, please if you can, do so but personally I can't, it is so deep within me". They decided to administer another dose of beating after which the same question was repeated. With agonizing voice, Rose replied that salvation was still in her and that it was impossible to leave it or take it out of her.

<blockquote>
Receiving salvation is free, but keeping it can be costly. This was the grim reality the girls soon came to confront.
</blockquote>

Finally, the school administration realized that flogging the girl as a disciplinary action was not yielding the expected result. They opted for another form of punishment. This time, Rose was given a punishment of cleaning the toilet sewage without gloves. They expected her to give up salvation because the punishment was even harsher than whipping. The place was exceedingly dirty and awfully stinking. To the amazement of her persecutors, Rose went ahead and cleaned the sewage with her hands without caring that she didn't have gloves. After this punishment, the same question of leaving salvation was asked. The answer was the same. Rose was not prepared to let go her salvation.

Unfortunately, as a result of the harsh punishments that Rose received, few among the students who had received Jesus as their personal Saviour became scared and renounced salvation. The majority, however, stood firm, refusing to let go the precious gift that they had received by God's grace.

The school administration assembled all students who refused to renounce salvation and told them off. They threatened them with suspension, or even worse, expulsion if they continued to be stubborn. The school wrote letters to their parents so that they could intervene to instruct their daughters to abandon at once the "confusing foreign doctrine of salvation" that invaded the school and advise them to concentrate rather on their studies.

Some parents wrote to their daughters telling them off and instructing them to abandon salvation. Rose' father also responded to the letter. He expressed his full satisfaction and gratitude to God because his daughter had finally received the Lord Jesus Christ as her personal Saviour.

"I have been praying for this, thanks be to God because He heard my prayers," Timoth wrote.

The school leadership was highly disappointed by the response of Rose' father. They finally gave up and stopped persecuting the born-again girls.

The Lord's Favour with the Born Again Girls in the School

The Lord's favour was with born again girls in this Secondary School. At the end of the school year, all born again girls without a single exception were at the top. They were the brightest students in the whole school. The headmistress and the teaching staff were amazed because their original understanding was that saved girls waste much of their time in fellowship, praying and studying the Bible.

From that time onwards, any girl who chose to be saved was not persecuted anymore for three reasons:

i.   The school management was convinced beyond any shadow of doubt that salvation had a positive effect on the academic performance of students.

ii. Born again students were the most disciplined. Due to the respect they had for God, they displayed excellent behaviour in the school. There was no need of applying any disciplinary measures against them because they were self-disciplined.

iii. The school administration had realized that any form of punishment, including flogging, could not take Jesus out of the hearts
of those who were resolutely devoted. Instead, persecution only
helped to strengthen their faith in Him.

Rose continued her studies in this Girls Secondary School. As she
was making considerable progress in her studies, she was at the same
time busy in season and out of season witnessing about Christ to her
peers. There was an exceptional anointing upon her life.

Never Leave the Lord Jesus

While still in the same Secondary School, Rose had another amazing
experience. The reader will recall that Rose' mum had died—that was in
1971. This time, Rose was still young pursuing her primary education at
Wanging'ombe School. Five years later, she had an unusual dream about
her mother. She narrates the story as follows:

*I had a dream meeting my mum. When I saw her, she
was in a very nice house made of glass. She smiled at
me, very pleased to see me. My mum called me and
said: 'Rose, make sure that you do not lose your salvation. Never leave Jesus Christ because I want you one
day to come where I am because it is such a wonderful
place.' When I woke up, I realized it was a dream, but
an unusual one. Today that dream is as clear in my
mind as it was that very day when I had it.*

*Some few years later, I had another dream. I saw my
mother again in the same building made of shining glass.
This time, she came much closer to me and told me the
same words she told me during the previous dream. As
she was talking to me, she opened the window of her
room a little bit. A wonderful fragrance that could not be
compared with any perfume I have ever come across in
this world gushed out of her room towards me and filled*

the place where I was standing. She tenderly touched me with her finger and cheered me to follow the Lord Jesus Christ all the days of my life. She then smiled and closed the window and that was the end of the dream.

When I woke up in the night, my body had the same fragrance as the one I smelt in the dream. The whole room was also filled with the same fragrance. When my fellow students woke up, they asked each other who had such a wonderful perfume but none had it. The fragrance remained in our room as well as on my body for many days. Finally, it slowly faded. This was absolutely amazing! I was tremendously encouraged to know that my mother was in heaven. This has always been such a source of joy and inspiration to know for sure that my mum did not perish, but rather lives a happy life with the Lord. The full assurance I have that one day I will meet my mum makes me happy beyond imagination.

Persevere, Never Give Up!

Rose is the seventh and last born in the Mangula family. Although she was always considered as a baby by all the other family members, Rose was always a source of encouragement to her brothers and sisters. One of her elder sisters, Theresa (not her real name) who is more than 20 years older than Rose had marital problems. She was married to a man who was not a Christian. This man used to take too much strong alcoholic drinks on a daily basis. As a result, he used to abuse Theresa several times, giving her a real rough time. It was a routine for Theresa to be beaten up by her husband. No single week could pass without being beaten.

Theresa, nevertheless, endured the situation for many years avoiding the divorce route for the sake of the upbringing of their children. She was determined to ensure that both of them as parents stay together to bring up their children. She hoped that the future would probably bring better days of stability for her family.

Unfortunately, as time went by, her husband grew from bad to worse. Theresa continued to suffer intensified domestic violence. As her husband became increasingly violent to the point that Theresa could not bear it anymore, she started considering separation.

On one occasion, after being violently assaulted by her husband, she made up her mind and decided to leave the husband. Many family members supported the idea as they could not see her future with that man. All those issues of separation were discussed among grown-ups. Nevertheless, Theresa decided to involve her little sister, Rose. She broke the news and told Rose that she was decided about separation from her husband.

Rose was 15 or 16 years of age when her elder sister shared with her about the decision to leave the husband and children following the unbearable domestic abuses from the man she married. Rose, in tears, took her sister aside and said, "My sister, I fully understand the situation you are passing through but do not leave your husband and children, instead persevere and be faithful even to the point of death, and God will give you the crown of life". Rose was referring to the scripture that she had read from the book of Revelation 3:10.

The Bible says that the Word of God is living and active; it is sharper than any two-edged sword; it pierces even to divide soul and spirit, joints and marrow. It is able to judge the thoughts and intentions of the heart (Hebrews 4:12). The words that Rose spoke sank deep within her elder sister's heart and bore immediate fruits. Theresa said, "Rose, because of the words you have spoken to me, I have now decided to change my mind and will endure the hard circumstances even if it means dying". She went back to her house and the situation didn't get any better. Whenever the abuses escalated and Theresa was on the verge of divorcing her husband, she always remembered the words that her youngest sister told her. Those words were always a tremendous source of inspiration to endure harsh circumstances.

As a result of her unwavering faith even in the midst of tribulations, Theresa was commended by her church to the level of eldership, believing that she would be such a great source of encouragement to many people. The husband also continued to be violent especially when under the influence of alcohol.

Guess what! After many years of hardship, a new chapter started in Theresa's life. Her husband repented and accepted the Lord Jesus as his personal Saviour. Theresa became the happiest woman in the village, living a wonderful life with her husband. The salvation of her husband also came with the recovery of the lost honeymoon.

Theresa could forget anything but not the words of encouragement that Rose spoke to her; words that initiated her new way of thinking; words that produced good fruits in her personal life and that of her entire family. Theresa's patience, faithfulness and prayers helped her husband to discover who Christ is and today he also has eternal life.

Today, Rose is an evangelist that preaches the Gospel of the Lord Jesus Christ in different countries. God has been using her in the ministry of reconciliation, bringing the message of hope to those who are discouraged. Obviously, I have had many opportunities of hearing Rose' messages. One of her most recurrent messages is entitled: *"Do not be discouraged, never give up"*. As this message was a source of comfort and encouragement to her elder sister more than 37 years ago, today it is still a source of tremendous help, a source of hope and encouragement to many discouraged people across the globe. *Never give up!*

The Far Reaching Effect of Testimony

In different schools, Colleges and army (National Service) where she passed through, Rose never gave up testifying about the love of God to mankind through His Son Jesus Christ. In fact, as days went by, her zeal for sharing with others about the Good News of salvation intensified. Preaching Christ and the pursuit of academic excellence were her two main priorities, in that order.

While at Rugambwa High School, Rose witnessed about Christ to her peers as she did in her former Secondary School. Many received Christ as their personal Saviour. One of them was Mat (not her real name). As a result of accepting Jesus in her life, Mat was disowned by her parents. They chased her from home a result of which she went to live with her uncle Dr. Max (not his real name), a well-known senior medical doctor in the City of Dar-es-salaam.

Dr. Max suffered a terrible disease that resulted into a sudden paralysis. The Tanzanian Health Ministry tried all it could for his treatment within and without the country. Treatments in different European specialized hospitals did not help anything.

After several attempts without success, Dr. Max decided to go back to Tanzania and wait for his day of departure from this world. As a medical doctor, he understood very well that all possibilities were exhausted, and that everything else was just a waste of time and resources. He was paralyzed and condemned to remain in a wheelchair all the remaining days of his life.

Dr. Max's critical health condition used to cause a lot of grief to Mat. She used to frequently and fervently pray for her uncle. Mat used to go to an evangelical church in Dar-es-salaam, but nobody else was a churchgoer in the whole household of her uncle.

One time, a crusade of a well-known Tanzanian evangelist Moses Kulola was announced at the Church. This evangelist was a powerful preacher and used to attract multitudes because of the peculiar divine gift of preaching the Word of God with clarity and power. God had also given him a powerful healing gift. During his crusades, the Word of God was always accompanied by signs and wonders.

Mat was scared to tell her uncle and highly learned cousins about the crusade as they used to mock her from time to time because of her faith. One day, as she was cleaning her uncle's room, she placed a copy of the crusade advertisement leaflet below her uncle's pillow and left the room. The uncle saw the advert leaflet, read it and threw it in the bin. The following day, Mat took the advert and put it again under the uncle's pillow. Dr. Max saw the same advert and threw it away again. When Mat did it the third time, her uncle was offended; he summoned the people in the house and asked who was putting strange leaflets under his pillow. Mat owned up that she was the one and apologized.

Mat's birthday was approaching. After a prayerful consideration, she approached her uncle and requested him to make her happy on her birthday. She told the uncle that the best birthday gift she would like from him was to accompany her one day to Evangelist Moses' crusade rather than taking her to a hotel for a meal or buying any other gift for her. The requested gift sounded ridiculous not only to the uncle but also to everyone else in the family. Nevertheless, in order to make her happy on her birthday, the uncle granted her request.

The day of the crusade came and the whole family was ready for the event. They drove their good cars to the crusade ground. While other family members joined the multitude to listen to the preacher, Dr. Max requested that his car be parked far away from the crusade ground. He did not want too much noise from loud speakers. He wanted to concentrate on reading his newspapers. He wasn't there because he was interested in what would transpire in the crusade but was there only to please his niece. Mat decided to remain in the car with her uncle so that she could be of any assistance in case he needed any. But that was not all. Her staying back was also strategic. She wanted everybody else to join the multitude so that they could hear the Word of God. She hoped and prayed that they be challenged and convicted by the Word and probably get saved.

The man of God started preaching a powerful sermon. While still preaching, something unusual started happening in the doctor's life. Dr. Max's temperature started rising followed by heavy sweating and intense shaking. He suddenly threw away the newspaper and started struggling stretching his legs and arms. Mat got scared thinking that the uncle was about to die. While she was devising a plan to run to the crusade ground and call the doctor's wife and children, Dr. Max opened the door and jumped out of the car. He started running towards the crusade ground leaping and screaming with joy, shouting that he was healed. He passed through the crowd and went to the front where the evangelist was standing. Everyone in the crusade wondered what was going on. The doctor's euphoria was distinctly discordant to what was going on. It could have been understandable if one chose to describe it as a commotion.

Dr. Max's wife and children saw *the man* who caused the commotion standing with the evangelist. Something was strange though: The *man* looked familiar—very familiar at that. Not very far from the evangelist themselves, they could see that it was Dr. Max but how could it be? They got confused, knowing that Dr. Max was completely paralyzed and unable to walk. Not only that, they had left him with his niece in his car a bit far from the crusade ground. They looked at one another, kind of asking unvoiced question: *Are you seeing what I am seeing?*

Dr. Max introduced himself to the preacher and told him about the wonderful miracle that the Lord had performed in his life. This was one of the biggest miracles that had taken place in that crusade and there was great rejoicing. In a state of awe, Dr. Max's family rejoiced tremendously after hearing the testimony of their beloved one. That day, many of them gave their lives to Jesus. As the reader would expect, this was a completely new chapter in the Max's family.

The news concerning this miracle spread quickly like a wild fire in a dry bush. In no time, it reached people in high positions of authority who knew Dr. Max. Before the end of the crusade, the ground was flooded with many Tanzanian top officials and hundreds of security personnel. They came to witness the miracle that had happened to Dr. Max. They were all amazed to see the restoration of a man who had lost hope of walking straight without crutches. He was completely healed.

As a result of this miracle, many Tanzanian officials and members of their families gave their lives to Lord Jesus Christ. Henceforth, Evangelist Moses' ministry in the whole country was boosted. He could preach the Gospel at any time and place with no official hindrance or interference. This was a wide open door for the evangelist to preach the Gospel to the whole nation.

Despite this amazing breakthrough for the preaching of the Gospel, the evangelist was confronted with strong opposition from 'unlikely' quarters—the other religious figures. But these oppositions did not yield much result since the man of God had found favour with God and the country's senior leadership. Any form of opposition was therefore bouncing back onto the face of his opposers. If God is on your side, no one can ever successfully be against you (Romans 8:31).

Amazing, isn't it? The effect of the Gospel preached by a young girl (Rose) born in Itandula, one of the smallest villages in Njombe district, to another girl (Mat) shook the entire nation of Tanzania. If Rose had not witnessed to Mat, Dr. Max could not have gone to the crusade, hence missing the encounter with God for his physical and spiritual healing.

And think about it! The story of Mat reveals the amazing divine operations. Mat was chased away by her own parents simply because she was saved. This was a mean act by her parents. Nevertheless, out of this despicable act, God worked a miracle in the life of her uncle who accepted her in his home. This reminds me of Daniel Ogweno's book: *"Taking a Reject Without Regret"*.

The chain effect of God's working through the lives of these seemingly *inconsequential* young girls did not end at Dr. Max's house. I mentioned above that Dr. Max's miracle was witnessed by senior political leaders of the country. Through this, the ministry of the man of God caught the attention of more people nationwide. With the resulting moral backing by some of these senior officials, more ground was covered in the whole nation. Thousands upon thousands, including government officials, were set free from the bondage of Satan. Even I myself got saved during Evangelist Moses Kulola's crusades. It is amazing!

> The story of Mat reveals the amazing divine operations. Mat was chased away by her own parents simply because she was saved.

Every Christian should be encouraged to witness to non-believers because we do not know how far-reaching the impact of that noble task would be for the benefit of mankind. You can lead someone to Christ and in future, this person may become one of God's generals or even the Head of State who would bolster righteousness in the country.

> For "Whoever will call on the name of the Lord will be saved."
> How then will they call on Him in whom they have not believed? How will they believe in Him whom they have not heard? *And how will they hear without a preacher?*...
> So *faith comes from hearing*, and hearing by the word of Christ. For whoever will call on the name of the Lord will be saved—Romans 10:13-14,17 (NASB, italics, author's emphasis).

The Breathing Bible

As explained in the previous chapter, Rose got saved and spirit-filled the same day. Having a strong Lutheran background, she completely repulsed any teaching related to water baptism. She believed that the sprinkling of water that was administered to her by the Lutheran pastor when she was a baby was enough. Her argument was that what mattered most was the spiritual meaning of baptism rather than the way it is done. Whether someone has been immersed in deep water or sprinkled with little water on the forehead made no difference to her. Even though she was a serious born again Christian, she categorically resisted any teachings to do with baptism by immersion. She did not understand why she should be baptized the "second time".

Despite her disobedience to the scripture, it was not lost on her that Jesus, the author of her salvation, was baptized by immersion in the river Jordan. But it was not a big deal for her. Rose continued preaching the Gospel of Jesus Christ with other university students.

One day, this young and dynamic group of university students visited a local church in Dar-es-salaam. The whole congregation was excited to receive in their midst young, energetic and learned witnesses of Christ. In his introductory word of edification, the pastor of the church was led by the Holy Spirit to talk about water baptism. He emphasized so much its importance for all believers and on the fact that baptism by immersion was the *only* biblical baptism. He emphasized that the Lord Jesus Himself was baptized by immersion in River Jordan.

These were teachings that Rose was not willing to hear. In fact, as the pastor was preaching, Rose fell into the trap of criticizing the man of God in her heart saying that pastors who are not highly educated put more emphasis on less important issues instead of concentrating on preaching the Word of God. This was dangerous because she wanted to bring in the level of education to have something to do with what was being taught. Abundant grace was however released unto this young lady who was zealous but lacking divine perspective on baptism.

As the preaching went on, the battle raged unabatedly in her heart. Maybe it was not that simple; maybe the level of education had nothing to do with it! May be the pastor was right!

Rose was holding her small Bible with her two hands. Suddenly, the Bible started 'breathing' — swelling and contracting. Rose compares the sensation she felt with those someone would feel when holding a living chick between his/her hands. She started trembling; her hands were shaking. People around Rose gazed at her and were stunned to see what was happening with her Bible and the way her body was vibrating. A still voice spoke to her, asking: *Rose! For how long will you resist my Living Word?* She immediately understood what the message from God was all about. In tears, she repented and decided to get baptized as soon as possible.

After that repentance and making a decision for total obedience, the breathing of the Bible and the vibration of her entire body stopped. It did not take many days thereafter before Rose got baptized by immersion. After the baptism, she experienced and became an even more fulfilled person; she had more freedom to minister to people of all denominations without skipping any biblical teachings.

A Vision on the Shore of Lake Tanganyika

Few years after her salvation, Rose had an unusual dream. She saw herself standing on the shore of Lake Tanganyika. For readers who are not familiar with the geography of the Great Lakes Region, Lake Tanganyika is located between the United Republic of Tanzania, Burundi and the Democratic Republic of Congo, not far from Rwanda. Its waters come from Lake Kivu situated between Rwanda and the Democratic Republic of Congo.

In the dream, Rose beheld someone drowning, struggling for survival. Rose perceived that the man was at the verge of giving up. It was apparent to her that the man was not a good swimmer. Gripped with exceptional compassion, Rose decided to do all she could to rescue that life. She immediately jumped into the water and swam towards the man. She got hold of him and swam back to the shore. The mission was successfully accomplished. She greatly rejoiced, feeling good that she had saved a life.

The rescued man appeared to be in his late fifties. He was blind in one eye. Rose felt compassion for the man's blindness even though it was just one eye. She felt an urge in her heart to pray for him. When she laid her hand on him and prayed, a miracle took place. The man's blind eye suddenly opened, he was then able to see clearly with both eyes.

Soon after the miracle, still in the dream, Rose heard a voice saying, *Rose, here is your husband!* Her immediate reaction in the dream was to rebuke that voice thinking that it was Satan who was trying to confuse her, but she quickly recognized that it was not Satan's voice but the Lord's. Nonetheless, in the dream, she still protested saying, *Oh No Lord! My intention was to rescue this man's life; I didn't do it in order to get a husband; I don't have to get married to him.*

She struggled in the dream trying to convince God that she did not want a husband, but rather to serve Him all the days of her life. As someone who was on fire for God, her thoughts always were to serve God only, nothing more, nothing less! Despite her resistance on the issue of marriage, the voice persisted saying, *Rose, here is your husband!* That statement marked the end of the conversation. The dream ended and she woke up.

She started wondering what kind of dream she had had. As she could not get any interpretation of that dream, she ignored it though it remained fresh in her memory. Amazingly, the dream kept on coming back multiple times on different occasions. It finally ceased but only after the picture of the man was permanently engraved in her mind.

CHAPTER 4

COLLEGE DAYS

*For one's life to be driven to the right destination,
intellect must be a passenger while godly devotion
must take the driving seat. And when intellectuality
is a student of spirituality, it confirms that indeed,
the fear of the Lord is the beginning of wisdom.*

A Courageous Soldier

At the completion of her secondary education (O-Level, comparable to GCSE in the British education system), Rose emerged among the top performing students. She was therefore selected to join Rugambwa High School in Kagera region for her advanced secondary studies, commonly referred to in short as "A-Level." This level is comparable to the Sixth Form in United Kingdom". This was a two year programme of study.

Towards the end of her A-Level education, just before the national final exams, Idi Amin Dada, the then president of Uganda invaded Tanzania and proclaimed Kagera region as part of Uganda. Rugambwa School was heavily bombarded by Ugandan Air Force. Reliable sources revealed that Rugambwa High School was targeted by Ugandan troops because it was mistakenly considered as part of the Tanzanian military barracks which were located within a short distance from the school. Fortunately, students did not suffer heavy casualties due to the swift and efficient intervention of the Tanzanian troops. They repulsed the invaders and evacuated all students to other schools, far away from Kagera region. After moving to a different school in Mwanza region, Rose sat for her A-Level exams. Her results were excellent.

Following the Tanzanian government policy for all students to do the National Service before joining any institution of higher learning or employment, Rose was sent to Mafinga and Oljoro barracks respectively for one year of military training. Towards the end of that training, Rose was sent to the front line in Uganda together with other soldiers. The Tanzanian government had decided to topple their enemy, Idi Amin, from power in Uganda. The Tanzanian troops had entered the Ugandan territory. Their presence was overwhelming. The Tanzanian troops were warmly welcomed by Ugandan citizens as *Wakombozi*, meaning "Liberators". The Ugandan people had suffered a lot from the ruthless regime of President Idi Amin. Tanzanian troops moved inside Uganda with a message of freedom and hope for the Ugandan people.

Rose was one of the soldiers sent to Kampala, the capital city of Uganda. She and her colleagues managed to enter the Ugandan State House and discovered a chamber where Idi Amin used to put corpses of his many mutilated victims. She says that many bodies were still in the State House. Once in the State House, one could easily sense an exceptional state of heaviness due to the presence of powers of darkness and the spirit of death.

After the downfall of Idi Amin Dada, Rose and some of her colleagues were called back to Tanzania and decorated with bravery medals by the Commander in Chief of the Tanzanian Armed forces.

Faced with Decision Making About Studies

After her military training, Rose was selected to join Makerere University in Uganda to pursue Information Technology. Only bright students who completed their A-Level studies with high grades were sent to Makerere for this course. This was a discipline that was new and highly marketable those days. She also had another offer to join the prestigious Mzumbe College in Dar-es-Salaam to pursue Hospital Management and Administration. Admission at Mzumbe College was also very competitive.

After a prayerful consideration, she found herself not interested in joining any of the two prestigious institutions of higher learning. Instead, God spoke to her clearly that she was to pursue a forestry course at Olmotonyi Forestry Institute where she would graduate with a national diploma in Forestry. She joyfully bowed to God's choice for her, rejecting other offers. Those who are led by the Spirit of God are the children of God (Romans 8:14).

When Rose shared her decision with her highly learned brothers and sisters, her choice looked foolish to them. They could not understand how Rose declined such exceptional offers that many people were struggling to get without success, and choose to go to a Forestry College located in a remote place in Arusha region.

Secondly, after two years of studies at Olmotonyi, she would graduate with a diploma while at Makerere or Mzumbe, she would graduate with a degree or Advanced Diploma respectively. To a common man, it was not easy understanding Rose' choice, but because she was resolutely certain that it was the will of God for her to go to Olmotonyi Forestry College, she decided to obey God regardless of other people's ideas and comments.

To the rational and informed mind, choosing a diploma instead of a degree is insanely ridiculous, but to a spiritual mind, the reasoning of man is not necessarily what carries the day.

In those days, forestry was not a popular discipline among ladies. This was because there was a tough practical side of it, especially because of its being menial. Only men used to be admitted in this course but when Rose applied for it, the first group of seven women were admitted and enrolled into this course.

Olmotonyi Forestry College is an international institute. Students from different African countries (Botswanans, Ethiopians, Malawians,

Zambians, Rwandans, Swazis, Tanzanians just to name a few) and Indians attended the College. The first group of Rwandan students was admitted into Forestry Course in 1977. These were sent by the Rwandan Government on Intercooperation scholarship, a Swiss based organization. I happened to be one of the five Rwandans to be admitted by the College.

When Rose joined the college, there was not even a single born again Christian in the whole campus. Personally, I was a registered member of the Rwandan Pentecostal church but living in sin. I was a Christian by name but not living a Christian life in any way.

When Rose and other six girls joined the college, all boys' eyes were on them. Imagine seven girls in a campus of hundreds of male students.

We noted something strange during the very first week of the academic year about these ladies. We could see seven ladies in the lecture room but during break and meal times, we could only see six. Students started wondering why the seventh lady was always missing during break or dinning times. The absent lady was Rose.

Before joining the College, Rose took sufficient time to intercede for the college. God revealed to her the spiritual decay of that college. As an ambassador of Christ (2 Corinthians 5:20), she fervently prayed to God for a clear strategy to use in order to promote the Kingdom of God in that College. God told her to abstain from witnessing or preaching to anyone in the college in the initial stages but start her life in that institution by prayer and fasting for seven days, interceding for divine visitation among students and members of staff. That is why she used to attend lectures but during breaks, she used to hide in one of the toilets and intercede for the work of God. She didn't eat any food during the first week of her academic life at Olmotonyi College. You could expect her countenance to be emaciated enough to cause people to wonder if she was sick or something. This, however, did not happen. During lectures, her countenance was normal.

After that week of intercession, the Lord told her to put on her badge on which was written, *"Jesus is the answer"*. When she came to the dining room for the first time with the badge, I remember students shouting, *Jesus is the answer! Jesus is the answer!*

Now, a debate started among the students, with some of them pejoratively asking: *If Jesus is the answer, what is the question?* As the debate went on, Rose started distributing some Christian tracts that had Good News of salvation written on them.

On a different occasion, when Rose was praying for the College, the Lord directed her to come to my room to witness to me and my roommate, another Rwandan national who was also pursuing a diploma course in the same college. When we saw her coming to our room, we couldn't understand what her mission was. We thought that she wanted friendship with one of us as it was the trend among young men and women on university/college campuses. Our interpretation of her visit was a corrupt one from corrupt minds, typical of sinners. Rose' mission was different. She had come to us on a divine assignment—to tell us about the love of God and His saving power through Jesus Christ. That was her mission from the Lord, nothing more, nothing less.

Within a short time, I had already discerned who she was. Although I was a sinner, my Pentecostal background helped me understand that Rose was not after any other worldly friendship, but rather was doing her Master's business as a seriously committed Christian. This discernment didn't come immediately to my roommate who had a catholic background. After Rose' departure, I told my roommate to be watchful about the girl, otherwise we could end up saved. We decided to cut communication with Rose and tried to avoid her whenever possible but she continued to show interest in us, always telling us about Jesus. We used to be embarrassed to be seen with her. Because of this, we used to do all we could to avoid her. Despite our obvious resistance to heed what she was telling us, she didn't get discouraged knowing what the Lord had told her about my friend and me. She continued praying for us and giving us Christian literature which we were not even interested in reading at all.

A Narrow Escape

Rose had a close friend, Tania, (not her real name). Tania's father had been terminally ill for some time. He was admitted in Kilimanjaro Christian Medical Centre (KCMC), located few miles from Moshi Town and Mount Kilimanjaro. At some point, Rose and some brethren felt that it was important that they visit Tania and her ailing father.

At the hospital, they met Tania at the corridor. She was in deep sorrow because her dad's condition had deteriorated. It was critical enough to make one conclude that he was about to die. For Tania, it would be a double loss if her father died without receiving the Lord Jesus as his personal Saviour. The pain of losing her father both physically and spiritually was too much to bear.

On different occasions, Tania had witnessed to her father about salvation, requesting him to accept Jesus as his personal Saviour. He had that far rejected the idea, terming salvation a "childish adventure."

Tania received the visitors and took them to greet her agonizing father and relatives who were with the old man. After greeting them, Tania and the visitors withdrew some distance away from the ailing father and relatives. They withdrew because it was not allowed that many people should flock around the patient around that time. They stood in the hospital corridor where they could see the patient and encouraged Tania to stand firm in the Lord and to continue trusting God for the physical and spiritual healing of her father even if his health condition appeared to be more critical. After a while, the old man opened his eyes and said: "Please call that girl for me!" "Which girl?" They asked? He said, "that one," pointing his finger to where his daughter, Rose and other brethren were standing.

The relatives thought that he probably wanted to talk to his daughter, so they called Tania in. The old man objected and said, "I want that girl who was standing besides Tania." The girl was Rose. Rose went in to the old man. Since the speech of the patient was almost gone, Rose didn't want to waste that opportunity. She immediately pleaded with him to accept the Lord Jesus Christ as his personal Saviour. To everyone's surprise, Tania's dad expressed his willingness to receive Jesus that very moment. Rose led him through the sinner's prayer of repentance and the man welcomed Jesus Christ into his life. Immediately, the face of the patient radiated with joy because he had made the greatest decision ever. Tania was overwhelmed with joy and thanked God for saving her dad. The following day, Tania's dad passed on and went to be with the Lord. What a lucky man! What a narrow escape! Like one of the thieves on the cross besides Jesus, Tania's dad received the Lord Jesus in his very last hours of the earthly life. He is now in heaven rejoicing with the Lord.

Not Yet Time to Go

One day, Olmotonyi Forestry College organized a student academic trip to Ngurdoto National Park. At the beginning of the journey, Rose distributed some Christian tracts to keep students busy, then she came and sat next to me in the bus. I felt embarrassed sitting with her knowing that she would definitely evangelize me all the way. What I anticipated did not actually happen. She only gave me and my colleagues some Christian literature (tracts) to read but there was no open discussion on God's stuff with anyone. Surprisingly, she was unusually quiet all the way. Before entering the national park, Rose' countenance changed as if something strange had happened to her. She was calm but with a deep pensive mood. She had had a vision of what was to happen to us that very day.

Rose says that it was her very first vision of that kind that took place when she was very much awake, her eyes wide open. She was quite used to divine dreams, but with this one, she was awake. The windscreen of the College Isuzu bus suddenly changed into something like a huge television screen and Rose watched events unfolding before her eyes as they were to happen shortly after. She saw our bus being involved into a terrible accident but due to her prayers, lives of all passengers on board would be spared.

After the vision, she was scared. Satan took advantage of her fear and tempted her to concoct a story to justify her decision to remain at the main gate of the park where there was an office and many Park's guards. Thanks be to God! She overcame the fear, rejected the devil's scheme and decided to proceed with all of us. We continued with our journey together but she was not as charming as she used to be. Unknown to us, she was involved in some spiritual warfare, interceding for the people on board. We finally reached our destination and did what we were supposed to do in that place. Lecturers explained what they wanted us to know. After this, we boarded the bus to start our journey back to college.

We had come to a sharp bend when the driver realized that the brakes were not working. He struggled to negotiate the corner in vain. He lost control and the bus immediately started rolling like a stone.

The slope was very steep and there was a small lake at the bottom of the mountain. I remember seeing the tragedy happening and worried that the end of everyone's life was at hand. As the bus was rolling, the velocity was increasing at an alarming speed. The bus had rolled three times when it suddenly stopped. It was hanging precariously on a tree that had pierced its body. It was damaged beyond any hope of repair. All seats were dismantled with exception of Rose' seat. All bus windows were broken into pieces except Rose' window. Lecturers and students were piled up in a heap in one corner of the shapeless bus.

To the amazement of everyone, only Rose was comfortable on her seat. As soon as the bus stopped rolling, people started struggling to find their way out. There was no guarantee that the tree would withstand the weight of the bus for much longer. The fear was that the bus would start rolling downhill any second. Frenzied, everyone was in a hurry to jump out. The ensuing pandemonium was itself posing a great danger. There wasn't enough space to manage the stampede and the uncontrolled surge of people meant that the bus would swing its weight on the tree thereby causing it overpower the tree sooner rather than later. But thanks to God! He had decided that what had happened was enough for the day, everyone came out.

Rose was the last person to leave the bus. People were shouting telling her to leave the bus as quickly as possible because the bus was swinging, but she held her peace and started collecting people's items (jackets, notebooks, pens and so forth) from the swinging bus.

As everyone else was in a shock and worried about what had happened, Rose was calm and peaceful. While the bus was rolling, Rose was engaged in spiritual warfare, praying loudly for safety of everybody on board. When she shared her experience with brethren, she said that her body was in the bus but her spirit was actually somewhere else. When the bus started rolling, she says that she was filled with extraordinary joy and then taken by the Spirit of God in another realm. This is the reason she explains that she did not even know how the accident took place except for what she had seen in the vision. She didn't feel she experienced the accident as it was taking place. She came back to her normal senses and found herself in a dismantled hanging bus while everyone else was already outside. She finally jumped out after collecting all items that were left in the bus. It was now clear to everyone that there was something extraordinary about this lady.

As the Lord had shown her in the vision, no death casualty took place. Everyone in the bus sustained different degrees of injuries except Rose. She didn't sustain a scratch.

There were a number of things that baffled everyone: The bus was badly damaged and yet no death occurred; how the tree was able to hold the bus until everyone was out! This was despite the anxiety and tension by frenzied passengers, making the bus swing even more on the tree; Rose' factor: her chair and window intact; her body intact; her composure extraordinary, especially considering that the bus was swinging and threatening to fall any second.

People started testifying that their lives were spared because Rose was in the bus. Christians, Muslims and Hindus to name but a few, all acknowledged the power of God that Rose worships because He spared their lives.

After the accident, the main problem was how to get assistance because it was extremely dangerous in that part of the park. There were signposts all over, warning tourists to remain on board of their vehicles for their safety because of many leopards and other dangerous animals in that particular area.

Even though the distance from the accident site to the main entrance of the park was quite long, Rose, being the only one who had no injury, decided to walk across the park so that she could report the incident to the park warders at the main gate.

After walking for about two kilometres towards the park's main gate, Rose met a Land Rover coming from the opposite direction. It had tourists and park guides. These people couldn't believe their eyes when they saw a lady walking unarmed and alone in a dangerous area of the park. The vehicle stopped and Rose explained what had happened. They took her on board and came to evacuate those who were seriously injured. As it was not possible to get other vehicles within the shortest period of time, those who were not seriously injured took the risk of walking to the main gate.

Faith Comes By Hearing

I was one of those who were slightly injured, walking towards the main gate. We reached a dark spot due to a high density of big and tall tropical trees. Something happened that I will never forget for the rest of my life. This was nothing but the conversation we had among ourselves. One funny Tanzanian student who was known for cracking jokes engaged us into a serious theme of reflection. He called the attention of everyone and said:

"Gentlemen, where are we now and where are we going? Everyone has witnessed how terrible the accident was and how the bus is shapeless and completely dismantled. Therefore, it is not true that we didn't perish. The truth of the matter is that everyone on board perished in that tragic accident. As we are walking together right now, believe me, we are not alive but dead. We are now on our journey to eternity. We are either going to heaven or to hell, but the fact that we are dead is irreversible. Now concerning this journey to our eternal destination, I doubt whether this is the way to heaven. The way to heaven is not as muddy as this and for sure it does not pass through thick forests with warning signboards about leopards and other wild animals; therefore I can assure you that we are on our way to hell".

After hearing our colleague's talk, we believed him that we were probably dead and fear gripped many of us. Our concern was that if we were dead and on our way to hell, then it meant that there were no more opportunities for repenting our sins and be reconciled to God. We started regretting why we didn't heed the voice of God when we were still alive and had the chance.

Thanks be to God! We were not dead. It was only a joke from a colleague but the message hit home. When I remember how we believed our colleague that we were probably dead, it helped me understand the scripture that says: Faith comes by hearing (Romans 10:17). We have to be careful about what we hear and how we deal with the information we receive. Everyone was scared after receiving the false message and it took us a couple of days to recover and believe that we were not actually dead.

As a result of the accident and the shock that ensued, everyone went to church the following Sunday. From outside, every one of us looked holy and for sure, sins were few that weekend. The service was attended by many accident survivors but none of us responded to the altar call on that Sunday despite the terrible experience we had during the week. Only some few individuals gave their lives to Jesus many weeks later. It is only Jesus who changes people's hearts and not adverse situations, accidents or even miracles.

The Incompatibility of Light and Darkness

Whenever light shines, the darkness has no other alternative but to give way. As children of God, wherever we set our feet, that territory becomes ours. We also pray and anoint our houses/rooms where we live and they become sanctified. Even when we are not there, nobody is allowed to mess up in our houses because they are guarded by holy angels. Anyone can decide to violate our property at his own risk.

In one of the colleges where Rose pursued her studies, she had a roommate called Nana (not her real name) who was not a believer. This young lady had a boyfriend, but she could not dare bring him into the room and misbehave whenever Rose was around.

Rose used to be away almost every weekend for church commitments in the nearby town. One weekend, Nana took advantage of Rose' absence and brought her boyfriend in the room. In the late hours (between 2 and 3am), loud voices were heard on campus. Everyone wondered what had happened. Nana's boyfriend had collapsed in the room and was almost dying.

Nana tried all she could to help him but in vain. She could not even help him to go back to his hostel because the young man was in agony. The girl had no other alternative but to inform her fellow students that she had a visitor in her room but he abruptly collapsed and she did not know what to do. The medical history of this boy showed that he had never collapsed before. Students in the same hostel woke up because there was commotion and loud noise in the hostel.

The news spread quickly like a wild fire on campus. Instead of sympathizing with the couple, students accused them of misbehaving in Rose' room, playing games that disturbed the presence of God in that room. These were students' speculations as no details of what actually happened were provided either by the girl or her boyfriend. But one thing was certain: the room was a special place because a child of God was living in it. Christians pray for their houses/rooms and anoint them the first day they move in. Rose had done the same for her room at the college.

Due to the overwhelming presence of God in that room, Rose' comrades used to weigh their words while in that room which they had nicknamed, "a holy room". A good number of deliverance sessions were performed therein and many folks also got saved in that room. Almost everyone on the campus believed that nothing belonging to the world of darkness could take place therein secretly without being exposed in broad light.

We are Not the Same

The forestry course involves many field practicals, within and without the campus. In some cases, practicals are conducted far away from college. Students have to spend many days, sometimes a week or even months, in remote places. During such practices, students get used to living under tough forest environments.

One time, Rose and her classmates went for a field practice for many days far away from campus. Students had to use sleeping bags on the floor of a room in a primary school located in a rural area. The room allocated for the girls had only one bed. The girls jokingly suggested that the only born again in the group, referring to Rose, could use the only bed available. The rest would sleep on the floor. They used to enjoy teasing and calling Rose names associated with Christianity or salvation. She accepted the offer and the other girls opted to sleep on the floor in their sleeping bags.

One evening, as students were taking their super, they got involved in a debate about Christianity. They asked Rose to provide tangible proofs that Christians are different from the rest. They also challenged her saying:

"Born again Christians get hungry just like non-believers; they eat the same type of food and, more, their skin colour doesn't change to radiate a certain peculiar glory after getting saved. Why then do Christians say that after receiving Christ they become new creatures?"

They sharply criticized salvation but Rose didn't want to get involved in much discussion. She, nevertheless, maintained that born-again Christians, even if they eat the same food; live in the same houses; attend same colleges as non believers, *etc*, they are new creatures in the Lord Jesus because their sins have been forgiven. The result is that they live a brand new life full of joy with a bright future for eternity. This reasoning was, of course, rejected by the students. After this debate, the students shifted to other topics of discussion until it was time to sleep in readiness for the work awaiting them the following day.

In the night around 2 am, Rose awoke—her sleep completely disappeared. Beyond any shadow of a doubt, she knew very well that it was the Holy Spirit who woke her up but she didn't understand what He wanted her to do. As she had not received any instruction from Him, she started guessing. She said to herself: *Probably the Holy Spirit wants me to pray, but I do not feel like praying because there is no specific burden in my heart. Furthermore if I start praying, I may disturb other girls and that would not be a good example to show as a Christian.*

After realizing that she had no specific burden on her heart to pray for, she thought that the Holy Spirit probably wanted to show her a particular scripture in the Bible. Since she did not have any lamp or torch, she got concerned that if she put on the lights, all the girls would be disturbed, they may wake up. This would not be any better compared with prayer. While still deliberating on what course of action to take, the Holy Spirit finally impressed on her heart to leave the bed immediately and put the lights on. When it became quite clear to her that the instruction was from the Holy Spirit, she decided to obey. She left the bed, walked toward the door and then put on the lights.

As she was walking back towards her bed, she saw a big snake crawling down towards where the girls were sleeping. Hurriedly, Rose opened the door, went outside and brought a big wooden stick. With all her energy, she hit the snake twice on its head and killed it. When the girls heard the disturbance in the room, they abruptly woke up wondering what was going on. Before Rose could explain what had happened, they saw for themselves a huge snake. That the snake was dead didn't mean much to them—they all started screaming. As expected, their screaming woke up the boys who were sleeping in other rooms. They scuttled towards the girls' room to find out what was happening. They found a huge snake that Rose had killed.

While everyone else panicked, Rose was relaxed and smiling. They asked how she knew that there was a snake in the room, she replied saying, "Before going to bed, I told you that born-again Christians are special people and you refused to believe me. Now if we are the same, why didn't you know that there was a snake in the house which was about to bite girls who were sleeping on the floor? Because I am a Christian, the Holy Spirit woke me up around 2 am. He instructed me to put on the lights and He showed me the danger that was about to befall the girls". She then spoke to them saying: "If it was not for the kindness of God, by now one or possibly some of you could be in a very critical condition after being bitten by the venomous snake." All of them praised the name of the God of Rose. Although they didn't give their lives to Christ, they all believed that Christians are peculiar people, different from non-believers.

A Seed that Does not Perish

On a different occasion, the same group of students had gone for forestry practicals far away from college. One young man who was a school-teacher in the area happened to know some of Rose' college mates who were his former schoolmates in high school days. One evening after work, he paid a visit to his friends. On his arrival, he was welcomed by his friends who also introduced him to other guys and to the ladies as well. As a young man, he was also interested to chat with the girls. As he engaged himself in the conversation with the girls in general and with Rose in particular, his friends called him and warned him secretly that he should not talk to Rose or be interested in her, otherwise he would be in danger of getting converted to Christianity. They warned him that the lady that seemed to be catching too much of his attention was a serious born again Christian who has the power of convincing people to become followers of Jesus Christ.

Boastfully, this young teacher told his friends that nobody could convert him. Rather than listening to his friends, he instead developed more interest of talking to Rose. His friends continued to warn him about more contacts with Rose but he assured them that he was not a cheap man to be converted by a woman to the point of getting saved and joining her religion. This man who was always wearing sun glasses even when it was not sunny, ignored his friends and continued to chat with the girls and with Rose in particular.

As it was always Rose' priority to tell people about salvation, she started sharing with him about the love of God and the benefits of salvation and reconciliation with the Creator. This man who was warned in advance by his friends was fully aware that such a message was to come to him any time from Rose. As he was on the alert, he told Rose straight away that he was not interested in such stuffs and advised her to proceed no further. After the conversation with the girls, he went back to his friends and told them about his time with the girls. When asked if Rose made the expected attempt to preach to him, he confirmed that she indeed told him about the love of God and the importance of salvation, "But as I told you, I am a hard guy, no woman can convince me to join her religious beliefs," he boasted.

The following weekend, that teacher visited his friends again. His main interest was to talk to the girls and possibly win one of them for a girlfriend. The first girl he met was Rose. She proceeded to ask him if he had the opportunity to think over the words she told him in his previous visit. She specifically asked him if he eventually considered getting saved. His reply had not changed from the previous one. He emphasized arrogantly that he was not interested in salvation and that nobody can make him change his position on this issue. Rose promised to pray for him. She actually prayed for him as God had put a heavy burden on her heart to intercede for this man.

While sharing with his friends who were concerned about his continued conversation with Rose, this man told them that what he said earlier still stood. "I told you I am not that cheap to be won to Christ by Rose," he said. "Even if she managed to win other people for Christ," he continued, "I am an exception. I do not belong in the category of people who can easily be converted by the words of a woman." The man was exuberantly confident and arrogantly eloquent.

After several weeks when Rose had even forgotten about him, something amazing happened. This man came to Olmotonyi Forestry College and inquired to be shown the hostel of his former high school mates. His friends came and were excited to see him. They asked him why he decided to pay them a visit without telling them in advance that he was coming so that they could organize and have some fun out of the campus. He replied that his coming was so urgent he had no time to plan for the visit. The idea of sending a message was not an option. He told them that he had to come urgently because he must meet the saved girl. He had even forgotten Rose' name. He was only referring to her as the saved girl. He requested if they could take him to the saved girl's hostel. This man who was holding a Bible in his hands revealed that he wanted to get saved and begged to be taken to Rose so that she may tell him what to do.

> The man was exuberantly confident and arrogantly eloquent as he declared that he cannot be converted by the words of a woman. He was wrong! It was the Word of God, not words of a woman.

With the exception of the visitor, everyone bursted into laughter. They couldn't withhold themselves. The visitor was not discouraged by the reaction of his friends. He insisted that he was serious about it and pleaded to be taken to the saved girl's hostel. Finally, his friends decided to take him to the girls' hostel. The boys knocked at Rose' door. When she answered the door, she was surprised to see a group of boys coming to her in the morning hours. Rose' fellow students told her that they were bringing her a visitor. "My visitor! Which one?" Rose wondered. "Yes, your visitor, this gentleman here," they answered. Rose couldn't recognize the man until they reminded her of who the visitor was. With laughter, the boys also added that the visitor had come to get saved.

Rose welcomed her fellow students and the visitor in her room. As she was too cautious and not comfortable to remain alone with the visitor in the room, she requested the other students to remain and give company to their friend. Without delay, the visitor started giving the full account of his story to Rose in the hearing of his friends. While narrating his story, tears started streaming faster than his words. When Rose remembered how arrogant the man was but now shedding tears before a woman and his friends, she realized that something genuine had happened in his life. The Spirit of God confirmed the same in her heart and that his tears were genuine—tears of repentance.

When this man's friends saw his tears, they were embarrassed. They all stood up, ready to leave, abandoning their friend in Rose' room. Rose requested them to remain for a short while. Without letting them know what she was doing, she cleverly went and locked the door and kept the key in her pocket. She did this because she did not want anyone to leave before the job was accomplished. She wanted them to witness the mighty saving hand of the Almighty.

While shedding lots of tears, this man shared his story as follows:

"Last night, around 2 am, I woke up from sleep. While wondering why I suddenly lost my sleep, I unexpectedly heard someone opening the door of my house. I had securely locked it before going to bed. I wondered who that could be. Then I heard his footsteps in the sitting room coming towards my bedroom. Perplexed about what was going on; I sat on my bed, eyes fixed toward the door of my bedroom. This person opened the door of my bedroom. As he opened the door, there was a great light in such a way that I could see the unexpected visitor. I was on my bed filled with awe, wondering what was next.

This visitor was a shining handsome man, but he appeared too serious—he was not smiling at all. He made one or two steps forward from the door towards my bed and stood there, gazing intently at me for sometime without saying a single word. Finally, he called me by my name and said, *Can you tell me why you ignored what this girl told you?* 'Which girl are you talking about Sir?' I asked. He then stepped aside and I saw Rose standing behind him, then the man came back to his former position in such a way that I could not see Rose again. That moment, I remembered every single word that Rose told me regarding giving my life to Jesus. I remained speechless—I had no answer to give. The man looked at me again for sometime without uttering a single word, and then he turned and left, leaving the doors open behind Him. The light that was shinning in the house vanished as he departed. I started wondering what was going on because what had happened was not a dream, but a real and tangible encounter with someone very special.

After his departure, I pondered on the words that Rose told me in general and the explanation she gave me on the urgency and importance of giving my life to Jesus in particular. That same night, as I could not sleep anymore, I decided to go to my neighbour who was a religious man. It was disturbing to knock at somebody's door at that hour of the night, but I had no other option because I needed comfort and answers to this issue of salvation. My neighbour woke up in amazement, wondering why I should knock at his door in the wee hours of the night. I told him what had happened to me and asked him how to be born again. Unfortunately, my neighbour had no satisfactory answer to my situation despite his religious background. I went back to my house disappointed and decided that I should come here at the College so that you could tell me more about how to get saved because I would like to give my life to Jesus now."

Rose led this man to Christ. He publicly confessed his sins, prayed the sinner's prayer and welcomed Jesus into his life. Rose prayed for him and dethroned the powers of darkness that had oppressed him for a long period of time. The supernatural power of God was in the room and His glory was present to the extent that this man's friends were amazed at the things that had taken place in their presence. They did not give their lives to Jesus that very moment, but with their own eyes, they saw the power of God and the saving grace of Jesus in action. The man was immediately changed and his face radiated with the joy of the Lord. Rose' prayers for salvation for that man were answered. The Bible says that the prayer of a righteous man is powerful and effective (James 5:16). The Word of God is a seed that never perishes. I have learnt from Rose the urgency of preaching Christ in-and-out of season. The Word of God can never return to Him without accomplishing His purpose (Isaiah 55:11).

Rose' visitor went back to his hometown, saved. He witnessed to various people and many of them gave their lives to Jesus. Today, the man is a fully committed witness of Jesus Christ in his home country of Tanzania.

A Young Woman of Faith

After the military victory of Tanzanian troops over Ugandan army, the victorious nation was hit by serious economic difficulties because the country had spent a lot in the war. Essential commodities in the country were scarce. The black market was rampant because the few available commodities were sold clandestinely and at exorbitant prices. Petrol was one of the most scarce resources. Travelling from one place to another was a big problem. People used to book bus tickets at a very high price and stay for weeks before travelling as only few buses were operating.

Rose left Olmotonyi Forestry College (Arusha) and went to Dar-es-Salaam, the capital city of Tanzania. Here, she was to meet a friend and then proceed to Mbeya where they were to attend a Christian conference that was due to start the following day. In Dar-es-Salaam, Rose was received by her brother and other relatives. She told them that she was on her way to Mbeya for a Christian conference. They told her that she should forget about it because transport had become a serious problem, especially from Dar-es-Salaam to different parts of the country. In fact, some of her cousins had booked tickets for several weeks to travel to Njombe in the southern part of the country but up to that very day, they had not obtained any breakthrough yet. This was one of the evidences that the transport crisis was critical in the country.

Few days earlier, Rose had been telling a young lady she had led to the Lord that all things are possible by faith. They had jointly agreed to trust God to open the door for them to attend the important conference that was due in Mbeya. They would travel by faith despite the transport problems in the country.

Rose told her brother and relatives that she acknowledged the seriousness of transport problems in the country but for their case, they would have to go because they were on an important divine mission. Everyone listening to her laughed and commented that sometimes saved people make jokes during obvious critical situations supported by tangible facts. Rose refused to accommodate those negative comments and went to the city centre to book and buy bus tickets. What she saw there was discouraging to the carnal mind. Queues of people waiting to buy tickets were extremely long. More than that, people were queuing for tickets to be used within the following two or three weeks. Therefore, to get tickets for people who wished to travel the same day was practically impossible.

As anticipated by members of her family, the situation was chaotic and Rose did not manage to get tickets and went back to her brother's house.

Her brother and relatives were waiting to hear the obvious that she failed to get the tickets, a proof that she was making too much of her faith. When asked whether she got the tickets, she replied that she has the tickets and that the bus would be leaving at 6pm. Everyone was amazed and said that it was a real miracle but none of them asked to see the tickets. As the time of leaving was drawing near, a taxi was called to rush them to the bus station. Due to heavy traffic, they were almost late.

The driver was already in the bus when they arrived. The engine was on and the bus could leave any minute. As Rose and her friend hurriedly approached the bus, the bus conductor asked them if they were travelling by that particular bus. This was a rhetoric question because one could easily tell that the girls aimed to catch the bus before it drove off. This must have been the reason the conductor didn't wait for them to answer. No sooner had he asked the question that he grabbed their bags, put them in the bus and requested them to hurry up on board because the bus was about to leave. He showed them where to sit and the bus left.

The bus was completely full. After some kilometers into the journey, the bus attendant started checking tickets from the back. When he reached Rose and her friend and asked to see their tickets, Rose said that they didn't have any but would like to buy them. The man did not ask many questions, he issued the two tickets at the normal price. They arrived at Mbeya on time, started the conference with others and had a wonderful time in the presence of the Lord. This was a miracle of faith. Faith is the assurance of things hoped for, the conviction of things not seen (Hebrews 11:1, NASB).

A Big Catch

When I went to Tanzania for my studies, I was a religious person. I knew almost everything about Christianity but was rebellious towards God's statutes. I was still living in sin. For the first two years, I was not even going to church except during vacation in Rwanda where I was known in my church as a 'good' Christian. Rose joined Olmotonyi Forestry College to do her pre-service diploma in Forestry when I was starting my third year.

I mentioned earlier that during the first week of her first academic year at Olmotonyi Forestry College Rose was always missing in the dining room. She was fasting and interceding for the college following God's own instructions. During this week of prayers, she was given strategies to follow in order to win the lost for God. I also mentioned the way she was led to come and testify to Laurian (my country mate) and I. Although we were touched by her testimonies, we did not immediately give our lives to the Lord Jesus.

In the meantime, a big evangelistic crusade was being organized by different churches in Arusha town. The preacher was a famous Evangelist, Moses Kulola. Rose invited Laurian and I to attend that crusade which was to take place on three consecutive evenings ($19^{th}-21^{st}$ January, 1981). Rose pleaded with us not to miss the meetings. On the first day of the crusade, we were there on time. The man of God, under the powerful anointing, delivered a very powerful message. One thing that surprised me, he was talking about my sinful life, and whenever he stretched his hand towards the crowd, it was as if his finger was pointing at me. I tried changing positions but still his finger would follow me.

I knew beyond any shadow of doubt that instead of playing games trying to change my positions, I needed to change my condition through giving my life to the Lord Jesus. But I decided to hold my ground. A small still voice told me to surrender all to Jesus, but the battle was raging in my mind. When the time for altar call came, many people including Laurian gave their lives to Jesus and were prayed for by the evangelist. At the end of the meeting, we went back to college. My colleague was rejoicing because of the greatest decision he had made of becoming a follower of Christ. I tried to be as cheerful as possible but my heart was heavy within me—I had no peace.

> I knew beyond any shadow of doubt that instead
> of playing games trying to change my positions,
> I needed to change my condition through
> giving my life to the Lord Jesus.

The following day, Laurian and I went again to the crusade for the second meeting. Again, the message was powerful but I resisted giving my life to Jesus despite the preacher's insistence, urging someone in the congregation to receive Jesus as his Saviour because his days were numbered—he would not be there the following day. Despite this imminent divine warning, I did not surrender that evening but went back to college disturbed and fearful.

Just as the man of God revealed during the crusade meeting, that night, someone who was in the meeting got involved in a tragic road accident and died. The following day, it was chilling and heart breaking to hear the sad news about the sudden death. I can't tell whether or not this person had surrendered his life to Jesus following the appeal by the man of God.

On the third day of the crusade, the preaching was still very powerful. Many people became Christians. The Word of God was accompanied by signs and wonders. Many sick people were healed and the demon-possessed were delivered, among other miracles. Finally, it was on this third day (21st January,1981) that I put aside my pride and stubbornness. I repented my sins and accepted the Lord Jesus Christ as my personal Saviour.

Rose was very excited about the most important decision that Laurian and I had made during Moses Kulola's crusade. A regular fellowship with her started and she was always concerned about our spiritual growth. Another young man whose name is Udoba also acknowledged the Lord Jesus as his personal Saviour. He joined our fellowship of three and we became a team of four hungry people who were really seeking the fellowship with God. Rose gave me a Bible.

The Word of God was so sweet to the point that whenever I started reading my Bible, it used to be hard to put it down.

A Strange Behaviour

Rose had a honourable performance. Because of this, after she graduated with the diploma, she was appointed to join the teaching staff of the same college as an instructor. She was in charge of soil science and botany subjects. Apparently, she enjoyed the teaching profession because she normally likes passing knowledge to others, not only in the academic arena but also in the spiritual matters and other spheres of life in general. Passing knowledge gives her inner satisfaction.

While teaching at the Forestry College, many people—believers and non-believers alike—admired Rose' personality as a girl and her firm stand in what she believed. As a lecturer, she fulfilled her responsibilities to the full satisfaction of her employer. Her motto was to do her work as unto the Lord (Ephesians 6:5). During weekends, she used to be busy with church activities, mostly in Arusha town. She had many responsibilities in the church.

It was quite a distance from College to Arusha town and there was no public transport linking the two places. Rose therefore had to walk 5 to 6 km on earth road to a place called Ngaramtoni where public taxis and minibuses were found. One could get to Ngaramtoni by following the road, but there was also a shortcut passing near a large forest plantation. Those days, this shortcut was not a managed road as it is today, but rather a footpath. Most of the time, Rose preferred using the footpath because it was safe, short and less dusty.

Without Rose' knowledge, a lecturer colleague of hers admired her so much, he desired to have her for a wife. Nevertheless, with full knowledge of Rose' stand as far as her faith was concerned, this man anticipated that if he proposed to Rose, it would be rejected because he was not a born again Christian. As he was determined to have her for a wife by hooks and crooks, he devised a scheme of marrying her by force.

It is unfortunate that this wicked practice still happens in some African countries. A girl would be kidnapped, taken far away and raped in the name of marriage by a man she doesn't love.

71

What actually happens is that the girl's movements are closely monitored for a couple of weeks or months. Once her routine is established, the so-called bridegroom prepares his car if he owns one or gets his friend's. Alternatively, he can hire a taxi. He also conspires with two or three of his closest friends and set an ambush where the wanted victim passes on specific days and times. As soon as she appears, the gang would grab her by force and shove her into the standby vehicle, with all precautions in place to prevent her from screaming. Her captors would then drive her away to the house of the so-called bridegroom who would rape her repeatedly and then declare that from that very moment the abused poor woman has become his wife.

This miserable and frustrated woman would be kept indoors like a prisoner for one or two weeks, the man consummating the "marriage" as often as he likes. Meanwhile, "marriage celebrations" would be going on at the clan level. News about her being "married" would circulate all over for those weeks she would be in captivity. Knowing that she is no longer a virgin and that nobody would be interested in marrying her anymore, the poor woman would finally surrender and accept to remain married to the man she did not love in the first place. This sounds crazy and barbaric in countries where human rights are respected, unfortunately, this practice is still in operation in some parts of the world.

> As soon as she appears, the gang would grab her
> by force and shove her into the standby vehicle.

Meanwhile, the parents of the "bridegroom" would send some gifts to the parents of the girl with a message of acknowledgement that their daughter is with them, safe and happy in the family that loves her. They would also present a formal apology and express their willingness and readiness to send a delegation from the clan to formalize the marriage by negotiating the dowry, among other cultural issues. The majority of people in modern Africa condemn this primitive and barbaric practice but it is not completely eliminated in few African tribes.

Sadly enough, this is what Rose' colleague, his level of education notwithstanding, had planned for Rose. This kind of practice was still going on in his tribe.

Thanks be to God for not allowing my wife-to-be to be ruined by that lot of uncircumcised heart. Without Rose' knowledge, they tried to capture her several occasions but without success. Whenever the ambush was set near the Olmotonyi — Ngaramtoni shortcut, the Holy Spirit would give her clear instructions preventing her from passing that way but rather follow the road. Whenever they had planned to wait on the main road, the Spirit of God would clearly tell her to use the shortcut. She had developed intimacy with God and she was very sensitive to the guidance of the Holy Spirit. As she was quite used to His voice, she was always obedient to Him without questioning. Those who are led by the Spirit of God are the true children of God (Romans 8:14). Also in the Gospel of John, it is written that the Holy Spirit will disclose to us what is to come (John 16:13, NASV). Other times, Rose would get a lift to town from college vehicles and would bypass that waiting gang with their car parked by the roadside.

Rose' story above reminds me of the biblical story about the king of Aram who was at war with Israel where God preempted the Arameans military strategies against Israel. God would reveal to Elisha what the Arameans were up to; Elisha would in turn inform the king of Israel.

> Now the king of Aram was at war with Israel. After conferring with his officers, he said, "I will set up my camp in such and such a place."
> The man of God [Elisha] sent word to the king of Israel: "Beware of passing that place, because the Arameans are going down there." So the king of Israel checked on the place indicated by the man of God. Time and again Elisha warned the king, so that he was on his guard in such places. This enraged the king of Aram. He summoned his officers and demanded of them, "Tell me! Which of us is on the side of the king of Israel?"
> "None of us, my lord the king," said one of his officers, "but Elisha, the prophet who is in Israel, tells the king

of Israel the very words you speak in your bedroom."
—2 Kings 6:8-12.

After trying several times without success despite precise information they were receiving from Rose' housemate about her weekend movements, they finally gave up and actually revealed their wicked agenda that had aborted countless times. While revealing their aborted plan, they actually testified and acknowledged the supremacy of God that Rose worships.

Christians are peculiar and most blessed people on earth because our God loves us so much, clearly speaks to us and we get the message on time. Our heavenly Father shows us where danger lies and we can avoid it and be safe to the amazement of those who spread nets and set up traps to capture us.

Broken Courtship

Rafiki (not his real name) was a dear brother in Christ. Besides his high academic qualifications as a civil engineer, this handsome and eloquent man was a powerful preacher of the Gospel of the Lord Jesus Christ. I remember one time, on invitation by our Christian Union, this young engineer came to Olmotonyi Forestry College. He preached a powerful sermon from the book of 2 Kings 5 about Namaan.

I remember how Rafiki eloquently described the power and authority of the Commander in Chief of the Assyrian Armed forces who, at the same time, was a leper. Everyone was amazed at the way he explained the story. From that day on, many students on campus used to call him "Commander in chief". Students enjoyed his preaching. Even non-Christians used to request the Christian union officials to invite the "Commander in chief" to come and speak to them again. Rafiki was a gifted preacher who knew how to deliver his message efficiently with exceptional eloquence.

As the reader may have already noted from Rose' evangelistic involvements, she was also a very dynamic servant of God. Together with the "Commander in chief", Rose would lead the praise and worship in a fantastic way and then the brother would come in afterwards and deliver a powerful sermon. Miracles used to happen as many people used to get their deliverance from demonic oppression. Everyone could see that the duo matched very well in the ministry.

As time went by ministering together, they both fell in love. The brother was attracted to Rose, he proposed to her. Rose responded positively. Everyone among believers who heard about it responded with an "Amen!" When I got the news about their engagement, I was glad and fully convinced the two would make such a powerful ministering couple.

According to her testimony, Rose agreed to be engaged to Rafiki based on how dynamic she knew him to be in the ministry but she did not take enough time to pray about it. Many people make irrational decisions about marriage simply because they do not take sufficient time to pray seeking God's guidance especially when the concerned people are born again Christians and active in the Lord's vineyard. We tend to forget that man looks at the outward appearance but the Lord looks at the heart (1 Samuel 16:7).

Matching in the ministry is good but does not necessarily guarantee matching in the house as a married couple. Of course, it is marvelous and desirable when married couples, according to the will of God, match in the ministry as well. Matching in the ministry alone is not a sufficient condition for a happy and stable family. It is imperative to seek the will of God until one gets clear guidance from Him before getting committed to someone for marriage.

After some months of courtship, God set a situation that awakened Rose to seek the face of God concerning her future marriage with her fiancé. It became very clear to her that it was not the will of God to marry Rafiki. She promised him to be a sister in the Lord, ministering together as usual, but without any plan for marriage.

Following the broken relationship, Rose decided to put marriage issues on hold for some time and concentrate more on serving the Lord in her youth as well as furthering her academic interests. These two were her main priorities. Marriage would come after completion of her studies.

CHAPTER 5

EVANGELISTIC TRIP TO RWANDA

Sometimes the visions of God are like a game of puzzle. It is until all the pieces are put into their rightful places that one is able to see the whole picture. Patience is key because more often not all the pieces are given at the same time.

Evangelistic Mission to Rwanda

The termination of courtship between Rose and Rafiki coincided with the time previously set for evangelistic mission to Rwanda. They were to come with other two brethren, a lady in her forties (today an ordained pastor) and another brother in his thirties who was a brilliant minister of the Word of God. Laurian and I had invited this team of four Tanzanian evangelists to come and preach the Gospel of the Lord Jesus in different churches in Rwanda.

Despite the disturbing recent termination of their courtship, the pre-planned mission to Rwanda went ahead without hitches. Rose and her former fiancé displayed exceptional spiritual maturity. They put aside the obvious pain of broken relationship and gave priority to God's business.

Due to telecommunication difficulties and unreliable means of transport between Tanzania and Rwanda, I was not aware of the exact time of their arrival in Kigali, the capital city of Rwanda. They had difficulties with their flight from Kilimanjaro International Airport to Mwanza due to many flight cancellations. They finally managed to fly to Mwanza. From Mwanza, there was no flight to Kigali, so they had to travel by bus. The journey was tiresome as it took a couple of days but finally they arrived safely in Kigali.

I was not in Kigali to welcome our guests but brethren, members of Kigali Pentecostal Church, gave them an enthusiastic welcome. Right away, they started ministering the Word of God. During their very first evening in the city, as they were ministering, God confirmed His Word by signs and wonders. When they laid their hands on new believers, all were baptized in the Holy Spirit. That night, there was great rejoicing among the brethren.

After ministering for two days in Kigali, a telegram was sent to me by their hosts, telling me that the visitors would be leaving Kigali heading to Kibuye town, the headquarters of my native province. The church in Kigali had organized how the evangelists would be received on the other end by the pastor of Kibuye Pentecostal Church. Those days I was not living in Kibuye town but rather at Gisovu, near the Nyungwe Natural Forest where I was working as a director of a Swiss funded forest project called Centre Forestier (CEFO) de Gisovu. It was some distance between Gisovu and Kibuye, probably 1½ to 2 hours drive on earth roads. On reception of the message, I quickly organized to travel to Kibuye to receive the visitors.

When the visitors arrived at Kibuye, they were warmly received by the pastor of the Kibuye Church. In Rwanda, when you receive brothers and sisters in Christ or any other visitor, the first thing to do as a Christian is to give thanks to God in prayer for their lives and safe journey. As the pastor was praying giving thanks to God for the visitors, the Holy Spirit confirmed in his heart that the visitors were true messengers of God and carriers of Good News. The Spirit of God whispered to the pastor saying, *One of these visitors is yours.*

The pastor did not understand what the Spirit of God meant by that statement. Rather than asking God in prayer what He meant by that revelation, the pastor understood according to his own interpretation that soon or later, one of the four would be a missionary to Rwanda. He looked at the two men wondering who would become the missionary. The pastor had already concluded in his heart that none of the two ladies was fit to be a missionary as one was in her forties and the other too young with academic and professional ambitions, as well as getting married at some stage and getting consumed by family responsibilities.

> When God speaks, what He means is not
> necessarily the immediate interpretation we
> may come up with. Sometimes it takes time
> to understand what God said some time back.

This reminds me of the fact that ministers are men like everyone else and can get it wrong some times, especially when they forget to ask the Lord for divine interpretation. The prophet Samuel got it wrong when he was on a mission at Jesse's house to anoint one of his sons as the new king for the nation of Israel. The Bible says that when Eliab stood before Samuel, the prophet looked at Eliab's stature and thought, "Surely the Lord's anointed stands here before the Lord, but the Lord said to Samuel, "Do not consider his appearance or his height, for I have rejected him. The Lord does not look at the things man looks at. Man looks at the outward appearance, but the Lord looks at the heart" (1Samuel 16:6-7).

The pastor did not share that revelation with anyone of them. Several months later when everything was then clear about what the Lord was referring to, the pastor shared with me what the Lord had told him. We marveled at the Lord's language that we many times miss despite His precision in whatever He says. Our failing is that we usually forget seeking His face for more details.

When I arrived at Kibuye, it was great meeting these four precious vessels of God. I took them to CEFO Gisovu at Wisumo. They had a wonderful time with brethren of our Christian fellowship and other churches in the region.

During their stay with us, the team behaved so well that neither Laurian nor I realized that the courtship between Rose and Rafiki was no more. They were all busy ministering to hungry people who were so eager to hear what God had given to them for the nation of Rwanda in general and the body of Christ in particular.

One afternoon, as Rose was cleaning around, the Holy Spirit spoke to her saying, *Rose, this is your place.* Rose understood very well that the Holy Spirit was speaking to her but she wondered what the message meant. As she was not grasping the exact meaning of the message, she made erroneous interpretation like the pastor in Kibuye. She assumed that the warm welcome received from the brethren at Gisovu and the exceptional hunger for God manifested by the people in Gisovu probably led the Spirit of God to confirm that she and her colleagues were at the right place, doing the right thing, and that God was prepared to do great things. Nonetheless, her perception and the resulting interpretation was not fulfilling. It left a question mark in her heart but she kept all this to herself.

The next trip we organized from Gisovu was to take them to various churches in the province of Cyangugu, south west of Rwanda. They ministered in many churches under heavy anointing. We actually spent more days in Cyangugu than had been planned. They returned to Gisovu on the evening preceding the day of their departure back to their country, Tanzania.

A Visit to My Parents at Midnight

My heart was troubled because, due to many evangelistic activities in Cyangugu, the possibility of taking visitors to my home village were becoming dim. Nevertheless, I suggested that we still go to my village as my parents were expecting to see them during their visit in the country as I had promised them. The visitors suggested the cancellation of the trip to my village. They wanted instead to proceed directly to Kigali, hoping that God will grant another opportunity in future for them to come back and meet my parents.

For some reason, I was sensing in my heart the urge to take visitors to my village but I did not understand why I had that strong feeling in my heart. I then suggested to the visitors to go through my village and then connect straight to Kigali without going back to Gisovu. This way, we would kill two birds with one stone. My humble guests consented with my suggestion. I had my jeep ready as we were to drive on rough roads. After supper, we set off for Ruganda, my village, located in Mwendo Commune/District. The distance from Gisovu to Ruganda was not that long (probably seventy to eighty kilometres) but it took us many hours to reach the village because the earth road was rough and slippery due to heavy rain. We arrived at my parent's house around midnight.

By the time we arrived, my parents were already in bed. They woke up and were very happy to meet the visitors in general and the one I used to describe as my second mum in particular, the one who led me to Christ and who did everything she could to feed me with appropriate spiritual food in my early age of spiritual childhood. This was none other than Rose.

Rose was very happy to meet my parents, but for some reason, she remained silent for some time, posing a deep pensive mood.

Guess what! When she saw my father, the Lord reminded her of the vision she had many years ago when she was a student in High School. The reader will remember the vision that Rose had, standing at the shores of Lake Tanganyika and seeing someone drowning in the lake. The picture of the man she rescued came back to her mind. Rose testified later that the man looked exactly like my father.

She became very troubled in her heart thinking that the team had made a mistake by being preoccupied with the work of God elsewhere but forgetting to spare enough time to be with my family. Rose lamented that my father could have been saved that same day had they come earlier. They could have had sufficient time with the family in order to lead my father to Christ. For her, this explained why I was insisting that they should see my parents before going back to Tanzania. She repented before the Lord for not sparing enough time for the old man because she was confident that my father's life was to be saved that day as she saw it many years ago. Her interpretation was shallow as the vision she saw had a much deeper meaning than what she thought. The vision was original and divine as we will see later. We spent between one and two hours with my parents and then we set off again for Kigali. The driving was tiresome but God provided sufficient strength. At least I was pleased that my visitors met my parents and prayed for them.

A Miraculous Trip Back to Tanzania

We arrived in Kigali during the early hours of the morning, around 5am. We were very tired because of spending the whole night travelling but the Lord renewed our strength and His grace was upon us. Our visitors were to leave Kigali by bus to Mwanza, Tanzania, the same day. From Mwanza they were to connect to Kilimanjaro International Airport by air.

The journey to Mwanza would take longer than usual (more than two days) due to transport difficulties. Rose and the other two brethren would be late to report back to work if they used the road. Laurian and I decided to bless our guests with air tickets to Mwanza as this would be more convenient for our friends, especially those who were civil servants. They were very pleased and quite grateful for the arrangement of travelling by air to Mwanza.

Arrangements for their flight in the afternoon of the same day with Air Tanzania were successful. Laurian offered to buy all air tickets for our visitors. We also agreed with Laurian that I would buy gifts for all visitors.

Apart from buying the normal gifts to our visitors, I felt in my heart that Rose deserved another special gift. With the knowledge that she was engaged to Rafiki and would get married soon, I strongly felt in my heart that the best gift to give her was a high quality wedding gown. I shared the idea with Laurian. As we used to call her our spiritual mum, the idea of beautifying her on her wedding day was highly supported by my friend Laurian. We took Rose to the wedding shop and I bought her the most expensive gown that was there. As the veil and gloves were not available at the moment, I promised to send them by post.

When they were about to board the plane, I presented the wedding gift to Rose and her "fiancé" and wished them a happy wedding day. They both received the gown with gratitude, and then we departed. As Rose was climbing the stairs of the aircraft, the Spirit of God spoke to her in a still small voice saying: *Rose, this gown will come back here.* She was surprised by that message but its real interpretation was still hidden from her.

As scheduled, the plane took off. When the plane was about to reach Mwanza, the aircrew apologized to passengers for the inconvenience, but the plane could not land in Mwanza. It was announced that due to circumstances beyond control, the plane was going to Kilimanjaro International Airport first and then to Mwanza thereafter. They promised that their stay in Kilimanjaro would be brief to avoid causing more inconveniences to the passengers destined for Mwanza. Time went pretty fast and the plane landed safely at Kilimanjaro Airport. Rose and her colleagues left the plane together with Kilimanjaro passengers.

Think of it! Rose and her three colleagues were the only passengers for Mwanza where they were to take another plane to Kilimanjaro International Airport. Now that God had miraculously intervened in their favour and gave them a quick lift so that after serving Him in Rwanda, they do not get frustrated by reporting back to work late, there was no point of being flown back to Mwanza. When they asked whether they should pay more money for bringing them to Kilimanjaro while their tickets were for Mwanza, the aircrew were rather apologetic for inconveniences. Rose and her colleagues were told that if they had chosen to end their journey in Kilimanjaro rather than being flown back to Mwanza, then they had nothing more to pay. They left Kilimanjaro airport rejoicing, thanking God for His divine favour. Within a period of less than an hour, they were already at their respective homes in Arusha town.

Divine diversion made a plane land at the right
airport, a special favour to four
God-loving missionaries.

Even now, whenever Rose remembers that miracle, she always marvel at the way God makes connections in favour of His children. He changed the plane's itinerary for the sake of His children. Rather than landing in Mwanza and then start the hassle of connections to Kilimanjaro of which there was no guarantee of getting the plane the same day, they were miraculously flown straight to Kilimanjaro Airport. What a mighty God we serve!

A Wedding Invitation With a Question Mark

Approximately ten months after the visit of the four Tanzanian evangelists to Rwanda, Laurian and I received wedding invitation letters from Rafiki. With great excitement, we opened the envelopes to see the venue and date so that we arrange our journey to Tanzania to witness and celebrate the wedding of our two friends.

When we read the details on the cards, we couldn't believe our eyes. The name of the bridegroom was Rafiki but the bride was not Rose but someone else, completely unknown to us. We were shocked and deeply saddened, wondering what could have happened between Rose and Rafiki.

We sent comforting messages to Rose for whatever happened that led to the termination of her relationship with Rafiki. We also requested her, if possible, to share with us what happened. When Rose replied, she did not give any detail of what happened but rather encouraged us to move forward in the Lord. She only said that marrying her former fiancé was not the will of God and gave us an assurance that both had no hard feelings about it.

CHAPTER 6

COURTSHIP

*Our whim may not necessarily be God's will.
Blessed are they who lay their whim on the altar of
God's will—ready to sacrifice it. Like Abraham who
got Isaac back after laying him on the altar for a
sacrifice, we might as well 'get back' our whim,
transformed into God's will.*

A 'Risky' Prayer of Faith

*A*s the director of the development Project, I was living in one of the biggest houses at CEFO Gisovu. This house had many rooms, but I rarely used to go beyond my bedroom, living room and bathroom. I was rare in the kitchen as I had a houseboy who prepared meals for me.

The big house increased my loneliness but even if I had a small house, it was time I felt I needed a companion for life. I decided to take some days in prayer and fasting, presenting my request to God.

Ask and it will be given to you; seek and you will find;
knock and the door will be opened to you. For everyone

who asks receives; he who seeks finds; and to him who knocks, the door will be opened. Which of you, if his son asks for bread, will give him a stone? Or if he asks for a fish, will give him a snake? *If you, then, though you are evil, know how to give good gifts to your children, how much more will your Father in heaven give good gifts to those who ask Him!* — Matthew 7:7-11 (Italics, author's emphasis).

The desire of my heart was to be led by God, first, to identify; then court and finally marry God's will for a wife. On my knees, I remember uttering to God what I call "a risky prayer of faith." I always wonder whenever I remember that prayer. Thanks be to God because I was talking to a Father who understands me more than anyone else. He knows me more than I know myself. He understood what I meant and gave me the best.

During my prayer and fasting time for a wife, I spoke to my heavenly Father in the following words:

Lord, this is the time I need a wife; a companion for life in this pilgrimage on earth. I have decided to come into Your presence for this important issue. I know You have many daughters, but it is hard for me to choose one of them as I do not know their hearts. My Father, please choose one for me but also consider my criteria in this matter about the kind of girl I would like to get from You. Whether she is black, brown or white, I will be happy with Your choice. Whether she is tall or short, learned or illiterate, blind or not, crippled or physically fit, may Your choice prevail. Nevertheless, one thing I strongly insist on, You know the hearts of Your people in general and of all Your daughters in this particular situation. Please give me a girl to marry who loves You with all her heart and who will continue loving and serving You without wavering all the days of her life.

I sealed my prayer in the Name of Jesus.

I prayed this prayer because I saw girls who seemed to be on fire for God before marriage, but then changed drastically after marriage, becoming worse than non-believers. As an individual, I was not prepared for such a disappointment in life of marrying and committing myself for life to someone who is not a genuine born again and committed Christian, who would not be prepared to serve God with me all the days of our life together.

> There is much more to a person than the looks and the physique. God's best would be my best as well.

After this prayer, the devil bombarded my mind with negative thoughts. He said to my mind:

Look here! You have made a serious prayer mistake. God heard every single word you uttered in His presence and He is going to give you a Christian girl to marry who is ugly, blind, uneducated and crippled. Get ready therefore, she is coming along your way soon because that is exactly what you spoke before God.

These thoughts troubled my mind for a while but the Lord reminded me of Matthew 7: 9-11:

> Which of you, if his son asks for bread, will give him a stone? Or if he asks for a fish, will give him a snake? *If you, then, though you are evil, know how to give good gifts to your children, how much more will your Father in heaven give good gifts to those who ask Him!* (Italics, author's emphasis).

After this scripture was prompted in my heart, I decided to resist the enemy. I commanded him in Jesus' Name to go away and leave me alone. Moreover, if God gave me an ugly woman to marry, He will equally give me enough love for her. An old adage goes: *Beauty is in the eye of the beholder.* And still, the so-called 'ugly,' may have the best 'inner beauty' there is.

About disabilities, the enemy should know that it is not a problem to marry someone who is handicap. The reason is that they are not second-class human beings. Whatever kind of woman God would give me, He would, together with her, give me what it takes to love her. He will give peace of mind and fulfillment in my heart. These are virtues of much more value than mere looks and abilities. There is much more to a person than the looks and the physique. God's best would be my best as well. Case closed!

Seeing that I had sealed the loopholes in my attitude—those attitudes that he could use to bombard me with negative thoughts—he gave up trying to approach me directly. But he was not done. He devised other misleading schemes. This time, he tried proxies—using some close Christian friends of mine.

Sam (not his real name), was a dear brother in Christ. Because he was my prayer partner, once in a while he would come to see me. One day, with excitement, he told me that he had great news for me. He said, "Brother Celestin, I have seen your wedding in a vision. It was colourful, quite exciting and the glory of God was manifest during the whole event!"

I asked Sam who the bride was because I got the impression that he also saw the bride in his vision. He replied saying, "I will not tell you, pray to God, He will show you the bride." I told him that there was no point praying and asking God what He had already revealed.

When I insisted that I would love to know my bride to be, brother Sam finally opened up and told me that my bride to be was Sister Claire (not her real name). Without special excitement but rather, in a relaxed mood, I told him that I would pray about it. Because I had told Sam that there was no need of praying and asking for what has already been revealed, my prayer would be seeking God to confirm if it is His will.

As we were talking, I could clearly see that Sam was shocked by the fact that I was not excited about the good news, but he made no comments.

The desire of my heart was to be led by God, first, to
identify; then court and finally marry
God's will for a wife.

I knew Claire, she was a good girl who loved God. A couple of months preceding the message brought by my friend Sam, I had had different occasions of meeting Claire in different Christian gatherings. I also had opportunities of praying with her and other brethren. My impression concerning her spiritual life and level of growth in the Lord were quite positive. She was moderately beautiful, physically fit and appeared to be a humble girl. Professionally, she was unqualified teacher. Interestingly enough, following the message brought by Sam, I started feeling attracted to her. According to my own judgement, Claire fulfilled the criteria I presented to God, taking into consideration especially her exceptional passion for Christ. Nevertheless, for some reason beyond my understanding, a small question mark kept on coming again and again in my heart whenever I thought about her.

I took time to carefully consider all factors that could be behind the persistent question mark. Only one thing seemed to stand out: Was it a result of Claire's low education? She was unqualified primary school teacher. I dismissed this argument because I had told God in prayer that the education level of my wife-to-be was irrelevant. But still, the small question mark persisted in my heart. I started rebuking Satan but it didn't work. The tiny question mark remained intact in my heart despite multiple rebukes to Satan.

According to my own judgement, Claire fulfilled the criteria I presented to God, taking into consideration especially her exceptional passion for Christ.

Some weeks later, as I was struggling with this confusing situation, brother Sam came to visit me again in my house. He told me that the same vision of my wedding with Claire came to him again. His description of the glory of God during that wedding was moving. Using human wisdom, the brother passed an indirect but strong message: *God was not happy with my disobedience.*

Sam had a lot of respect for me, that is why he didn't challenge me directly and charge me with disobedience to God, but I got the message anyway.

Without my friend's knowledge that I had actually started appreciating the girl in my heart, I calmly gave him the same answer as the previous time that I need more time for prayer. I invited him to continue praying about the issue for more guidance from God. He didn't understand why we should continue praying for something that the Lord had already revealed—I had told him as much myself, he must have been getting confused as well. He instead advised me that we should be giving thanks to God for great things He had done.

Despite Sam's second message reinforcing the previous one, the struggle in my heart didn't end. As I said earlier, I appreciated the girl and I was almost 99% willing to marry her, but only a very small percentage was not in complete agreement within me. Meanwhile, I continued meeting Claire in Christian gatherings and prayer meetings but I avoided showing that I was getting interested in her. On her side, I could see that her conduct before me had changed from what it used to be. I could see from afar that she had some interest in me but she tried everything she could to hide it.

Claire's home was approximately 50 kilometres away from my work place, near a small town called Kibogora (a home to a big hospital, many schools, churches, development projects and tourist sites on the shores of Lake Kivu). I frequently used to go to Kibogora for administrative, medical, social or spiritual activities. I had also preached in Claire's church twice or thrice.

As I continued praying about Claire, the Lord didn't tell me anything more because He had already replied using the persistent small question mark in my heart. I had not realized that it was God speaking to me. I was rather wasting time rebuking the enemy thinking that the persistent question mark was from the devil.

Brother Sam brought me the same message about marrying Claire for the third time. My reaction was still the same as in the two previous occasions. When my friend Sam realized that I was not making any moves, he became discouraged and finally gave up. He neither brought any other message about the subject nor held any other conversation with me about Claire. Externally, I appeared calm and relaxed, but inside, a serious battle was raging. I was getting concerned that I was disobeying God after sending three messages with an "answer" to my prayer for a wife.

One night, as I was pondering about the whole issue, I decided to move to action because despite that tiny question mark in my heart, the love for Claire was growing in me and I knew that she also admired me. Not only that, I could not see anything contradicting the criteria I presented to God in prayer. I therefore decided to pay her a visit and propose to her. The night before my journey to Claire's home, I decided to spend a considerable time before the Lord in prayer and committing my journey into His hands. Since the small question mark still lingered in my heart, I earnestly made another special prayer, saying:

> *Dear Lord, you know that I love You. I have this journey tomorrow to meet Claire. If it is not Your perfect will, please let me know so that I cancel it right now. Alternatively, if I go tomorrow and it is not Your will, please stop me on the way. If You already communicated with me that it is not Your will but I didn't get it right, please forgive me. In case I go ahead and propose to Claire against Your will, please prevent this marriage from taking place even if it is only a day before the wedding. Please do not let me go ahead with something contrary to Your perfect will.*

Imagine the kind of prayers I used to utter before God! God to cancel the wedding even if it is a day to the event! My prayers were bold and daring. I was hungry for God's will, nothing more, nothing less. God is merciful. He looks at our hearts and evaluates how sincere we are with Him. He knows that we are only children. After that strong prayer, I went to bed.

The following morning, around 10, the car was ready for my journey. I didn't want to be driven by anyone; therefore my driver had an unexpected day off. I only took on board a young mechanic trainee so that he could assist with changing tyres or any other small mechanical issues that may unexpectedly arise. After a short prayer, I set off.

The road to Claire's house branched left off the main road at Kirambo shopping centre, two to three kilometres before Kibogora town. At Kirambo, instead of taking the road to Claire's home, I felt urged in my heart to go to Kibogora first, greet few friends and then proceed to Claire's home on my way back. In my initial plan, I was set to meet Claire; there was nothing like going to Kibogora first. The idea came when I arrived at Kirambo, when I was just about to branch left towards Claire's home.

On my way to Kibogora, I met my close friend Laurian. We both parked our cars on the roadside and started chatting. It was nice to meet him after many days. Laurian was working at Rangiro Forest Station in Cyangugu Prefecture (Province) far away from CEFO Gisovu. In the process of chatting, we shared testimonies about the goodness of the Lord. Just from nowhere, Laurian started sharing with me about being very careful with various decisions we make in life because many times we tend to go ahead of God and end up in serious problems due to operating outside the will of God. He really stressed on that point that we should avoid making decisions hurriedly and wait upon the Lord and His timing.

On hearing my friend's words of wisdom, I lifted my hands in reverence to God and worshipped Him for answering my prayer. Laurian was surprised and wondered why I was so excited and thankful to God. According to him, he had shared nothing new or special with me but simple words to edify one another. I decided to share with him the reason of my mission for that day. I told him the way my original itinerary suddenly deviated on my arrival at Kirambo shopping centre and decided to go first to Kibogora.

Laurian was one of my friends I would have liked to meet. It was indeed a divine appointment to meet him without any effort of looking around for him. I proved to him how God was behind all those changes as it was important to meet him first before committing blunders. I thanked my friend for the divine message he shared with me. I knew beyond any shadow of doubt that God had clearly spoken to me through my friend Laurian. The visit to Claire was cancelled that very moment and I decided to go back to Gisovu.

On hearing this, Laurian was troubled in his heart. He told me that he had no message for me from God and pleaded with me to go ahead with my mission. Laurian knew Claire as a good girl who believes in Jesus and who lives a practical Christian life. He felt sorry about her and did not like the idea that I changed my mind on the basis of the words of edification he had shared with me. Nonetheless, it was no longer possible to reverse my decision despite Laurian's avid encouragement to go ahead with my original plan. As far as I was concerned, God had clearly spoken to me and the message had sunk deep in my heart.

My friend came on board my vehicle and the mechanic trainee joined Laurian's driver in his car. We drove to Kirambo shopping centre and had a meal together before driving back to Gisovu. On my arrival at home, I took some time to thank God for the way He answered my prayer I innocently prayed the previous night. It was not God's will for me to propose to Claire. I fully understood the reason behind the small question mark that was always in my heart whenever I thought about Claire. It became quite clear to me that Claire was not meant for me but for someone else. By His abundant love and concern, God stopped my move at the right time before proposing to her against God's perfect will.

Few weeks later, Jack (not his real name), paid me an unexpected visit at Gisovu. Jack was a good friend of mine, someone I respected. Besides being a committed Christian, Jack was also a senior official in public administration at Kibuye. On his arrival at Gisovu, my guest was excited and more joyful than usual. He was bringing a special message to me. He told me that while praying for me, God showed him a sister in Christ who was to become my wife. He told me who the girl was. I will refer to her as Claudine (not her real name).

By the time Jack broke the news to me, I had met Claudine only once at Kibuye town during a Christian conference. Claudine was a born again Christian and a government official in one of the administrative districts of Cyangugu Province. Her home was not very far from Jack's home in Cyangugu and they both belonged to the same local church.

Claudine was absolutely beautiful. In terms of external beauty, there was no comparison with Claire. Surprisingly enough, after getting the message from Jack concerning Claudine, my heart was repulsive and I became disturbed in my heart about the whole issue. At least with Claire, the question mark in my heart was tiny but with Claudine, the question mark was big and unsettling. It was as if there was a huge traffic red light ahead of me flashing forth, warning me not to move any further. I thanked my friend Jack for the message, kept it in my heart but never acted upon it. I did not even take time to pray about it because the answer was quite clear in my heart. Despite her exceptional beauty and being a sister in Christ, she was not for me.

One time, Jack and I decided to visit some Christians in the Democratic Republic of Congo, formerly called Zaïre. We planned to pass first at Jack's house to greet his family. Before reaching Jack's home, we coincidentally met Claudine on the way. She was walking on the village road. We stopped and parked the motorbike on the roadside in order to greet her. In the Rwandan culture, when friends meet, they hug each other especially if they have not met for many days. Jack and Claudine hugged each other the normal way we do in Rwanda and then came my turn. When Claudine gave me a hug, it was more than a hug as it lingered much longer than usual. She was not willing to let me go to the point that I wondered what was going on—could there be a saying: *he hugs longer who hugs last?* We chatted for few minutes, then we proceeded with our journey.

After we parted from her, Jack commented about the 'enthusiasm' with which Claudine greeted me. He interpreted what he saw as a kind of confirmation of what he had told me when he visited me at Gisovu. He said with confidence that definitely something good will happen in the near future between Claudine and me, assuming that the special hug I received was probably a product of God's revelation to Claudine about our future life together.

I did not comment anything because it was not the story I was willing to hear. My heart was miles away from her and I was not prepared to entertain any relationship with her as the red light was still flashing in my heart. I only smiled at Jack's comments and that was the end of the story. I never had any correspondence with Claudine and from that day onwards I never saw her again. She only used to send greetings through Jack. When she realized that there was no response from my side, she obviously understood that I was not interested in any special relationship with her beyond being a sister in Christ.

The different messages I received from my two friends, Sam and Jack, concerning two different ladies, each of which was to become my future wife, put me off and raised many unanswered questions in my heart. It was obvious that something was wrong with those revelations—I doubted their sources. If they were from God, there was no way He would offer me two different ladies, not to choose from but each one of them was to be my wife.

I presented the whole situation to God in prayer and decided to relax in His presence till His appointed time. I told Him that in due time, He would give me a wife according to His own choice. Meanwhile, I was not going to pray about it anymore but give thanks to Him because I would soon find His choice.

Although I had initially felt that it was time to get a wife, I decided to slow down a bit lest I 'move ahead of God.' When I made that decision, God helped me not get preoccupied with the need for a wife by convicting me that there were other urgent issues to be prayed for, especially in the work of God. I decided to consider the issue of getting married as a normal thing that will happen in its time, but not as a priority for that particular moment. From that time on, I concentrated on the work of God; on my official duties as a project manager as well as other issues that required my attention.

In Quietness of Heart, God Speaks

After eight months or more without praying for a wife but rather busy with my work in general and God's work in particular, God revealed to me who was to become my future wife. This was none other than Rose. Beyond any shadow of doubts, God confirmed this to me in many ways. These can make a book of their own.

At the beginning, when God started showing my life with Rose as husband and wife, it was not easy to accept it because the idea of marrying her had never appeared in my heart before due to the following two main reasons among many others:

Firstly, I had always considered Rose as my spiritual mother because she is the one who technically led me to Christ, and I honoured her in that capacity. After being born again, she fed me with the spiritual milk and food until I grew up and was able to stand on my own in the Lord. Therefore, the idea of marrying my spiritual mother had never found a place in my heart.

Secondly, Rose was a foreigner who could not speak any of the languages spoken in my country. In Rwanda, we used to speak French and Kinyarwanda while Tanzanians speak English, Swahili and other tribal languages. It was quite clear that communication would be a major barrier. Of course, she could easily communicate with her husband because I speak English and Swahili but it would be a real problem to communicate with her in-laws and other people.

In view of the above arguments among many others, I classified this revelation about Rose marrying me as another distraction that the enemy was bringing up again. In fact, I resisted the idea several times, taking it to be an attack from the enemy. The more I resisted the idea, the more unprecedented special peace about the whole issue flooded my heart as God multiplied irrefutable revelations to me. God did not send anybody to tell me about it. He knew that I would not be ready to listen to anyone anymore following the previous misleading revelations I received from my two friends, Sam and Jack. God preferred to speak to me directly and I knew beyond any shadow of doubt that Rose was God's perfect will for me.

Obviously, during our college days in Tanzania, I had always considered that blessed would be the man who would marry her due to her outstanding spiritual qualities and zeal for God, but it had never appeared to me that I would be the blessed man—some things could be too good to be true.

Even after becoming convinced that Rose was God's choice for me, I still found it overwhelmingly intimidating to break the news to her—I struggled. My assumption was that the previous wounds she suffered as a result of the broken relationship with Rafiki would bring her to think that I was taking advantage of the situation. I therefore kept a low profile about it for a period of over a year. Besides this, I was also wondering how to introduce the marriage topic to someone I used to call my mum and respected as such.

God Broke the News

The battle was raging in my heart. This time the problem had nothing to do with confirmation whether Rose was God's choice for me or not. I was one hundred per cent sure that she was the one, but the problem was how to break the news to her about the whole issue. God impressed in my heart to tell Rose about it. I knew very well that it was God instructing me to do so, but for some reason, I was taking too long. I clearly sensed in my heart that the delay was an act of disobedience to God.

One day, I went to Kigali for official duties related to my work and spent the night at the Episcopal Church Hostel in Biryogo. The Spirit of God impressed in my heart to write to Rose and propose to her. I took a pen and paper but missed the courage to write what was in my heart; instead I bought a postcard with beautiful scenery showing Lake Kivu and the imposing mountains of Kibuye region. Instead of writing the exact message about marriage as it was boiling in my heart, I rather copied Psalm 23 as it is in the Bible. The message on the postcard was written as follows:

Dear Rose,
Be blessed by the following words of this psalm:

> *The Lord is my shepherd; I shall not be in want. He makes me lie down in green pastures, He leads me beside quiet waters, He restores my soul. He guides me in paths of righteousness for his name's sake. Even though I walk through the valley of the shadow of death, I will fear no evil, for You are with me; Your rod and your staff, they comfort me. You prepare a table before me in the presence of my enemies. You anoint my head with oil; and my cup overflows. Surely goodness and love will follow*

*me all the days of my life, and I will dwell in the house
of the Lord for ever.*

God bless you. Greetings.
Celestin.

Without putting the card in the envelope, I only affixed the required stamps and posted it. After posting the card, I felt a sense of guilt in my heart. A still small voice told me in my heart that I disobeyed as I did not do what I was supposed to do. As I was not having more time of staying any longer in Kigali in order to write the appropriate letter, I asked God to forgive me and promised to write the exact message as soon as I arrive at Gisovu. Within the same week, I wrote the letter proposing to Rose and posted it one week after posting the postcard.

One day, when Rose was in her office at Olmotonyi College, the office attendant distributed letters from the post office to different offices as usual. Rose also received her mail that included the postcard I had posted a week earlier. She picked up the card and read the message. You will recall that I copied Psalm 23 on the card as it is in the Bible, word by word. Surprisingly enough, Rose read a completely different message from what was actually written on the card. When I heard this testimony from her, I couldn't believe my ears. I was surprised by the marvelous doings of God.

The message that Rose read on my card was a message of love and appreciation, a message pledging to marry her. After reading that message, Rose became upset, not by the content of the message but rather by what she called "lack of wisdom". She wondered why I wrote such a delicate message on the card and did not even think of putting it in the envelope. She was concerned that the office attendant and other members of staff read the message on the card and therefore they would spread the news all over that a certain Rwandan guy is pledging to marry Rose. She feared that this would become the main topic on the campus news headlines.

But that was not all! Besides being upset with me, she was also gripped by compassion, thinking that probably something had gone wrong with my head. From the way Rose knew me, she was confident that in my normal senses, I was not the kind of a person who would have written such a message and make it accessible to the public unless something had gone wrong in my head.

Rose felt the urgency of writing back to me with motherly guidance based on Holy Scriptures and at the same time send a gentle rebuke for lack of wisdom revealed by writing such an important and confidential message on an open card that could be seen by many people. Another main issue of great concern was about the name of the Lord. Many people on campus knew that we used to pray together as born again Christians. She was concerned that people would think that our plans were to get married rather than salvation issues.

Disturbed by what people on the campus would start talking about, she decided to leave the office and go home. She wanted to be alone without office disturbances so that she could write a strong letter to me. As soon as she reached her house, she took a pen and paper, sat on her bed ready to write. She did not know when she fell asleep and when she woke up, it was morning of the following day. She was surprised and couldn't understand what happened. Her pen and paper were lying on the bed. All the same, she didn't give up her resolve to write. She was determined to send a strong correctional message that would 'help' me in life. Before doing that, she went back to her office, picked up the card to read it again. To her great surprise, the message she read the previous day was not anywhere on the card but Psalm 23. Rose was shocked and wondered what was going on in her mind. She looked at the message once again, it was Psalm 23. An important question arose in her mind asking herself from where she got what she read the previous day. She wondered whether she was normal or becoming confused. Rose slowed down the idea of responding hastily but decided to take time before God in prayers.

The message she read on the card was exactly what I was supposed to have written instead of Psalm 23. God was not pleased by what I did. He decided to break the news to Rose using His supernatural divine method and the recipient got the exact message. One week later, as Rose was still in a state of awe seeking the Lord about the whole issue, she received another letter from me. She was absolutely surprised that the exact message she read on the card was now written on paper. She couldn't understand how she got the exact message one week earlier before the arrival of my letter.

Despite the stunning proof with the card that clearly showed the hand of God in the whole issue, Rose found it difficult to get married outside the boundaries of Tanzania, in a foreign land. Being the very last born in her family, she found it hard to go far away from her father. In her culture, the last born has more responsibilities of taking care of his/her parents in their old age.

After considering all factors that were going through her mind, she decided to write a letter to me and gave it to Mr. Phenias Biroli, the then Director of the Rwandan Forestry Department who was on official mission in Tanzania. Rose met this man in Arusha town where both were attending an International Forestry Conference. After realizing that Mr. Biroli was a Rwandan who knew me, Rose decided to give him a letter for me. Mr. Biroli promised to pass it to me as quickly as possible. The letter contained some doubts. Keen analysis could easily see that Rose was not ready to marry me. When Mr. Biroli came back to Rwanda, he put the letter in one of the drawers of his office desk and forgot to give it to me.

As far as Rose was concerned, the answer to my proposal was "No!" Following the termination of her courtship with Rafiki, she wanted more time before getting engaged to someone else. She had purposed to use more years of her youth in the service of the Lord. Another hindering block was her desire to complete her university education before considering any issue related to marriage.

One day, Rose went to Arusha town to meet Paulina, a servant of God, one of the four Tanzanian evangelists who previously visited Rwanda with Rose. Paulina and Rose were so close to each other in such a way that Rose used to treat her as her mum. During their conversation, Paulina asked Rose if someone else had come forward to propose to her after the termination of her relationship with Rafiki. She replied that many had tried their luck but she was not prepared to entertain such matters with anyone. She maintained that marriage at that particular moment was not among her priorities. Paulina was interested to know the names of those people who had proposed to her for marriage. Rose told her the names of those who had approached her. Some of them were known to Paulina. They included pastors, university lecturers and engineers, to name but a few. Rose added that everyone was coming saying that God revealed to him that she would be his wife. As Rose could not accept that God could reveal one girl for marriage to many men, she rubbished all those revelations, qualifying them as mere distractions from Satan. "It is not possible to be married to many men and that is why I decided to tell all of them that I am not ready for marriage at the moment" she said.

Paulina asked if the list of those who approached her for marriage was exhaustive. "Yes!" Rose replied. "Are you sure?" Paulina probed. "Yes!" Rose replied, but at the same time, she wondered why Paulina seemed not convinced that the list was complete. Rose tried to remember all other people who had approached her. After some time, she finally remembered the forgotten one. She told Paulina that she forgot to mention another one but this one was not even on the list of those she would consider for marriage due to many obvious factors, therefore the answer for this one is a categorical "No!" Paulina was interested in knowing the fellow whose name was deliberately omitted from the list of those who had proposed to Rose. "It is Celestin, that young man from Rwanda," Rose replied. Paulina asked Rose if the "categorical No" to Celestin's proposal came up following times of prayers on the subject.

"You are a serious born again Christian who taught many people including myself that prayer should precede every decision-making regarding important issues, therefore you teach what you do not practice," Paulina charged. "Did you pray first before concluding that he is not the one?" She probed further. Rose replied, "Mum, I have many issues to pray about but not that one. There are some obvious issues to pray about and you can sense the witness in your heart to pray for those issues. I am not urged in my heart to pray about Celestin's proposal due to many obvious factors such as social and cultural differences; geography; communication, just to name but a few. You know that Celestin is not a Tanzanian".

Paulina rose like a lioness and rebuked her saying, "Rose, it is utterly wrong to reject something without taking it seriously before the Lord in prayer. I am not telling you that the man from Rwanda is the one you must marry, but I am not happy the way you handled this issue and I believe God is not happy either that you can afford to take important decisions without seeking His position." She rebuked that attitude and challenged her to seriously take the issue to the Lord in prayer before writing to me. Paulina had a clear revelation from the Lord that Rose and I would get married but she didn't want to tell Rose directly. She wanted her to pray to God so that He speaks to her personally.

Rose received Paulina's challenge with a positive attitude and decided to take a week of prayer seeking God's direction on the subject. In the midst of her prayers, God plainly spoke to Rose and said:

> *Rose, it is my perfect will that you get married to Celestin, therefore do not resist my will. I want you to know very well that I am not sending you to Rwanda for marriage alone, but also for a specific mission that I want you to accomplish for Me in that nation.*

At the same time, God also reminded her of the dream she had many years ago while standing on the shores of Lake Tanganyika. God also brought to Rose' remembrance the way she was resisting the marriage issue with the man she had rescued from drowning. This was exactly what she was doing following my actual proposal for marriage. This became the turning point in Rose' attitude towards getting married abroad. She fell on her knees, cried to God with tears of repentance. As Mary said to the angel Gabriel (Luke 1:38), Rose also said, "I am the Lord's servant, may it be to me as you have said."

Yes, But Cyprus First!

Immediately after spending the whole week in prayer, she wrote to me saying "I have taken your marriage request to the Lord in prayer. He has confirmed that it is His perfect will that we get married, therefore my response to your request is 'Yes!' Nevertheless, I already have a five-year scholarship to study in the University of Cyprus and all arrangements for my departure have been finalized. Would you be ready to wait for a period of five years?"

Oh! That would be like an eternity of waiting, but if it was the price to pay to marry Rose, so be it!

My reply was simple and straightforward. I thanked her for the reply and confirmed that I would wait for that period. In fact, I even encouraged her not to interrupt anything but rather go ahead with her plans. I assured her that I was prepared to wait, not only for five years but also for ten if that was the will of God.

Rose was expecting that I would probably protest saying that five years was too long, but she was surprised by my encouragement and readiness to wait not only for five years but even longer if it was necessary. This sounded unusual to her because men who want to get married normally object to a long waiting period. She again presented the issue before God and said:

"Father, I know that it is Your perfect will that I get married to Celestin. On the other hand, You have opened a door for me to further my studies in Cyprus and You provided a scholarship. Many people wanted this scholarship but Your favour was upon me and I got it. It is now too late to cancel all arrangements for my departure to Cyprus. Again, even if I cancel my studies, it would be too late for the scholarship to be given to someone else and this would anger my sponsors. They would be annoyed with me for such a disappointment and that would not be a good testimony as a Christian. Therefore give special grace to Celestin to wait at least for five years before we get married."

> This sounded unusual to her because men who
> want to get married normally object to a long
> waiting period.

On my side, I also took time to give thanks to God for confirming to Rose that she was to become my wife. About the waiting period, I spoke to God in prayer with honesty that my desire was to get married soon but if it was His will for Rose to go to Cyprus for five years, I told God that I was willing to wait for any period of time. I only asked Him for His grace during the waiting period, assuming that God would be giving me an important lesson on waiting. I was fully prepared to submit to His will. Strange enough, within me, I had no witness in my spirit that the Cyprus project was the right one for Rose at that moment in time but I didn't want to push anything.

The time was drawing near for Rose to leave but shortly before her departure to Cyprus, a serious war started in that country. The war was so devastating that the Tanzanian Government had to cancel Rose' scholarship for security reasons. She was instead told to join the University of Dar-es-salaam, in her own country. Rose was encouraged by her learned brothers and sisters to take the offer, but she made her mind to decline the offer. She was afraid of falling into Jonah's trap of taking the wrong direction from the perfect will of God for her life. She chose to get married.

Rose took that decision after reviewing all signs and messages she received from God with full assurance that our marriage was in His perfect will. The following were some of the confirming signs:

- The mind blowing issue of the postcard;
- The rebuke from Paulina and her encouragement to take everything to God in prayer;
- The voice of God that spoke to her confirming that our marriage was in His perfect will with a clear message that God was not sending her to Rwanda for marriage alone but also for another important assignment for the glory of His Holy Name;
- The way war suddenly broke out in Cyprus.

There were many other signs that God showed her which are not mentioned in this book, all were very helpful in her decision-making. She also remembered the vision on Lake Tanganyika that God showed her when she was still young, a time she had no thought at all about marriage, and many other signs confirming the same. After considering all these signs, she decided to decline the admission and scholarship offer to the University of Dar-es-salaam. She temporarily suspended her academic ambitions and preferred to be married first. Her relatives couldn't understand why such an unwise decision, but she had already made up her mind and that was final.

The Final Test

Up to this stage, Rose had not shared with her father about her friendship with me. This was a result of the long distance between her home in Njombe District (Southern part of Tanzania) and Olmotonyi Forestry College, her work place, located in Arusha region (Northern part of Tanzania). To go home, she had to travel by bus over 400 miles (660 kilometres) from Arusha to Dare-es-Salaam and then 450 miles (approximately 720 kilometres) from Dar-es-Salaam to Njombe. It was quite a long distance. Also there was a serious problem of telecommunication in Tanzanian rural areas. Practically there were no telephones in the remote parts of Tanzania. More than that, in the African culture, letter writing and use of phones are not normally preferred as a means of discussing marriage issues, especially with the father. These require face-to-face conversation. Therefore, Rose decided to travel to Njombe to meet her dad and tell him about the whole story.

Even though Rose had received all convincing signs from God, her father's position was also important for her. Before travelling, she told God in prayer that if her father accept and bless the idea without struggling, then she would take it as a final sign. In case the father rejects the idea, then she would have questioned the whole issue as she was not prepared to get married without her father's blessings.

It doesn't matter how many times we test the Spirit of God if our motive is to get things right in order to proceed with full assurance that we are walking in God's perfect will. He would be patient with us.

Rose travelled to Njombe and had an interesting fellowship with her father. She broke the news about her friendship with me. She said, "Dad, I have a friend who proposed to me but this man is not a Tanzanian but a foreigner. What do you say? Should I go ahead or turn down his request?"

Without showing interest in knowing which country that foreigner comes from, the father looked intently at Rose and asked her whether she was still saved or not. "Yes dad, I am!" She replied. The father responded, "If you are still saved, did you pray about it and if you did, what did God tell you?" Rose replied that she prayed about it and God confirmed that it was His perfect will to get married to that man, nonetheless she informed her father that she also had to consider other factors such as the impossibility of taking care of him in old age as it is the custom in their tribe that the last born has more care-taking responsibility over the aging parents than his/her other siblings.

Due to the long distance separating the two countries, Rose expressed her concern that it would be difficult to take care of him if she went very far away. But her father replied:

"If God confirmed that your friend is the right man for you, who am I to oppose God? I would be concerned and disturbed if the whole issue was not in the perfect will of God. If you are sure that your friend is God's choice for you, you should not ask yourself unnecessary questions. Concerning the issue of him being a foreigner, I want to remind you that God created all men. It is very wrong to discriminate among the people of God. You have my blessings; you may go ahead with your plan for marriage".

During her conversation with her father, Rose enjoyed favour before God and her father. The father repeatedly blessed our marriage project. Rose did not need any other sign as what she had received from the beginning of this relationship till that very day were more than enough. She was now ready for marriage. We went ahead and started preparations for our great day.

The Dowry

A dowry in African culture is something very important in marriage. Its size varies from one tribe to the other and from one region to the other. In some places, the dowry can be very expensive, between two and fifty cows. Some parents prefer monetary equivalents. I was prepared to pay the dowry but I had no idea about the amount of money required or the number of cows I was to give as a dowry. I was waiting for information from my family's delegation that was to go to Njombe to formalize the marriage request and to negotiate the dowry.

My family's delegation was headed by Pastor Steven Melisheki of Kaloleni Pentecostal Church (Arusha) and also included Pastor Paulina and other two gentlemen. They were warmly received by Rose' father and other members of the family. They officially presented the marriage request to Rose' family. They followed this by discussing other requirements. At the end of their mission, they came back to Arusha with a good report. Rose' family had given their blessings for the marriage.

Concerning the issue of dowry, to my great surprise, I was told that Rose' father declined receiving any dowry. He said that he agreed with his wife when she was still alive that they should not 'sell' their daughters for dowries, therefore he couldn't dare violate the agreement he made with his wife. He strongly underlined that the only dowry they both required from their sons-in-law was to love their daughters with all their hearts and live peaceful lives with them.

To cut the long story short, I did not pay any material dowry, but I sincerely love my wife and my love for her grows as days go by. Her beauty never fades. I have always enjoyed a peaceful life with this woman and we both give all the glory and honour to God.

CHAPTER 7

LIFE TOGETHER: AT HOME AND IN THE MINISTRY

The virginity and beauty that greeted the inauguration of life, not to mention the magnificence and abundance of providence, were not meat enough to satisfy Adam's soul. Therefore, in His divine discretion, God gave him a help meet to be his soul mate. No more evenings without Eve!

A Special Bride for Me

The 11th day of February 1984 is a special day in my life. This is the day When God joined us as husband and wife. When we met in the church for our nuptial blessings, Rose was shining almost beyond recognition—you wouldn't be blamed to take her for an angel, arriving right from heaven.

The wedding ceremony was officiated by Reverend John Njaghaga of Kaloleni Pentecostal Church in Arusha town (Tanzania). The presence of God in the church was overwhelming. The marriage drew multitudes—invited and non-invited; nationals and internationals; Christians and unbelievers; Muslims and Hindus.

Mr. Chungu, a Muslim who attended our wedding made the following statement in Swahili language after the wedding ceremony:

"Ukweli ni kwamba, katika harusi ya Celestin na Rose, mgeni Yesu alikuepo. Harusi bila mgeni Yesu ni kupoteza muda."

His statement translates as follows: "The truth is that during the wedding of Celestin and Rose, there was a special guest called Jesus. A wedding without Jesus as the guest is a waste of time". Mr. Chungu continued spreading the same message at his home village of Wangingombe in Njombe district of Iringa region. He testified to his friends about the divine glory he experienced in our wedding. It was not lost for him that all this glory was due to the special guest called Jesus. And why not! Jesus was a special guest and, as expected, speaker after speaker acknowledged Him. After a couple of months, one of his Muslim wives who also attended the wedding gave her life to Jesus and became a Christian. Praise God!

Coming back to our wedding day, before going to bed, we had a time of fellowship and prayer for a life together that had just started. We shared the Word of God laying the foundation on Holy Scriptures that would guide us during our long journey together on earth. I gave her one of the special gifts I had prepared for her. This was a Bible written in the language spoken by her in-laws and citizens of her new country. This was prophetic in the sense that she was on a mission to take the Gospel of the Lord Jesus Christ to the people of Rwanda in their own language.

As a Tanzanian who had never lived in Rwanda, she was obviously not able to speak Kinyarwanda, but now she was holding the Kinyarwanda Bible that she was to use proclaiming Good News to her new people. After this, I was led in my heart to anoint her with the precious oil I had bought from Rwanda for that purpose. After this long fellowship, we went to rest.

"Please God, prevent my womb from
carrying anyone who would end up in hell."

At this juncture, I do not want to be silent as many people usually do. Rather, I want to take this opportunity to challenge men who say that virgins do not exist any longer. I also challenge girls who accept to be compromised through illicit and fraudulent sexual intercourses before marriage due to lies that no virgins exist in the world anymore. Those poor girls shamefully lose their virginity, a precious gift that they were to present to their future bridegrooms during the first consummation. They pollute, undermine and give away the precious blood of virginity. This ought to have been the blood of the covenant of marriage shed during the very first sexual intercourse with a husband. The knowledge about this blood covenant is a mystery and known to few people.

In the same measure, it is a wonderful thing for a man to give his wife the gift of masculine virginity. It is a great feeling for a woman to know that she is the first and the only woman that you have known in the Biblical language. Unfortunately, due to the masculine sexual drive, especially among adolescents who are also driven by curiousity, many boys give away their virginity. This is more so among those who don't grow up under the watch of committed parents. It is important for believing parents to emphasize to their children the importance of keeping oneself unpolluted by illicit sex.

Now to those men and women who believe that virgins no longer exist, I challenge you. Rose was a virgin! I found her brand new. She had kept herself pure. To those who are keen observers, you'll see that Rose has two rings on one of her fingers. One is the normal wedding ring I put on her finger on the wedding day; the second was bought few days after. I placed it on her finger as a sign of honour because I found her virgin.

A Prayer for Children Before Conception

Rose and I love children so much. Immediately after our marriage, we took time to give thanks to God for our union and for children that He would give us according to the parents and pastors' blessings. In our prayers, we placed a request before God that we would not like to give birth to children destined for hell but rather to populate heaven, therefore in case any of our children would not inherit the kingdom of God, we earnestly asked God not to allow him or her to be born. Even if it means having no children, then let it be so rather than giving birth to people who would not reach heaven at the end of their lives on earth. I vividly remember when it was Rose' turn to pray, with her hands on her womb, she said, "Please God, prevent my womb from carrying anyone who would end up in hell."

We made a covenant with God that if He gives us children, then it means that they would be people who would inherit the kingdom of God. We thanked God for our children and trusted Him that our children would be mighty men and women of God who will hold high the banner of Jesus Christ across the nations. As per our humble prayer we presented to God before their conception, we strongly believe that none of our children will be a hell casualty.

What a Humble Lady!

Rose is a humble lady who knows the One she has believed. Humility is one of her key characteristics that challenged me most. True humility comes from God and if the Spirit of God lives and operates in someone's life, obviously the fruit of the Spirit will manifest in that person.

> By their fruit, you will recognize them. Do people pick grapes from thornbushes, or figs from thistles? Likewise, every good tree bears good fruit but a bad tree bears bad fruit. A good tree cannot bear bad fruit, and a bad tree cannot bear good fruit.—Matthew 7:16-18.
> Make a tree good and its fruit will be good, or make a tree bad and its fruit will be bad, for a tree is recognized by its fruit.—Matthew 12:33.
> No good tree bears bad fruit, nor does a bad tree bear good fruit. Each tree is recognized by its own fruit. People do not pick figs from thornbushes, or grapes from briers. A good man brings good things out of the good stored up in his heart, and an evil man brings evil

things out of the evil stored up in his heart. For the mouth speaks what the heart is full of.—Luke 6:43-45.

One day, Rose made a simple mistake—I hadn't even realized it. Saying sorry for it would have been more than enough. But in the evening, she came where I was and knelt before me and said, "My husband, please forgive me because today, I made a mistake." Since I was not even aware of what she had done, I feared that it must have been something big. When she told me what it was, I was amazed at how small a deal it was.

Her remorsefulness and the gesture of her humility following this small matter humbled me just as much. Her act of humility melted my heart and increased my love for her even more. I held her hands, lifted her up and stood her on her feet. I then gave her a hug of love. As I held her in my arms, she was glad, shedding tears of joy.

Easy Adaptation in New Environment

Rose grew up speaking English, Swahili and Kibena languages. Following our marriage, she had to move to her new country, Rwanda, where French and Kinyarwanda were the mainly spoken languages. Obviously after our marriage, she faced serious language barriers. It was difficult for her to communicate with her in-laws. From time to time, my mother was longing to converse with her to express her warm welcome, love and appreciation to her daughter-in-law, but it used to be hard due to language barriers. For the first 3-4 months of our life together, Rose was condemned to talk to me alone, unfortunately I was rare in the house due to my official responsibilities as the Project Director. Whenever I was available, she used to take advantage of my presence to maximize learning new Kinyarwanda vocabularies and how to pronounce them.

At the headquarters of the project at Wisumo (Gisovu), by the grace of God, we had managed to start a Christian fellowship. We used to hold weekly meetings in which many people received the Lord Jesus Christ as their personal Saviour. During these meetings, I always availed myself to translate for Rose.

One day, when Rose was to preach, it happened that I was not around. Brethren were worried about what was going to happen. She confidently told the leader of the meeting that she would preach in Kinyarwanda. Rose had started making simple Kinyarwanda sentences but they were cumbered by many mistakes and wrong pronunciation. Because of this, the leader of that day's meeting wondered how she would preach in Kinyarwanda for the first time.

When the preaching time came, Rose stood up by faith. To the amazement of everyone, she started preaching in Kinyarwanda. Although she made many grammatical mistakes, the message was clearly delivered. More than that, the boldness she had of preaching in the language she had just started learning, was a good sign of courage and full determination of knowing her new language.

From that day onward, she experienced a special breakthrough with speaking Kinyarwanda. I never translated for her anymore but encouraged her to keep on preaching in Kinyarwanda. She quickly learnt to correct grammatical mistakes as well as catching the right pronunciation. Within a short period, she built confidence in speaking the language. She could then sit for hours and hours talking and laughing with her mother-in-law and the rest of the family as well as with brethren and neighbours.

Today, I sometimes laugh when Rose and I visit the family in Tanzania. The Kinyarwanda is deep-rooted in her to the extent that when talking Kibena with her relatives, sometimes she unknowingly switches to Kinyarwanda. I have to keep on reminding her that she is speaking Kinyarwanda to the people who do not understand it.

As Rose was learning Kinyarwanda, she was concurrently learning French. She has not yet mastered French as she did with Kinyarwanda but she is not worse off. Learning French was interrupted by other academic undertakings.

The Healing of My Father From Spiritual Blindness

While in my office at Crête Zaïre-Nïl Development Project, I received a telephone call that my father was ill and hospitalized in Biguhu Health Centre. I was not that much worried because my brother, as a medical professional in charge of the Health Centre, was doing everything possible to give the best care to our father. Nevertheless, I decided to travel to Biguhu to visit my father. When I arrived, I realized that his condition was so bad and my brother was concerned about the whole situation. In fact, my brother had decided to transfer him to Kilinda Hospital where he was to be examined and treated by specialized doctors.

The following day, my father was transferred to Kilinda Hospital where he fell into a coma and stayed in that condition for a week. His condition was growing from bad to worse. As there was no hope for my father's recovery, doctors suggested that he be taken back to Biguhu Health Centre because it was near many family members who could easily visit him during his last days. After hearing the doctors' report, another scenario of transferring him to Kigali Referral Hospital flooded my mind. I asked the doctors to give me a detailed report concerning my father's condition and sought their views about whether transferring him to Kigali Referral Hospital would be of help in any way. The doctors told me frankly that transferring my ailing father to Kigali would not help in any way because the situation was terminal. They strongly suggested that we take him back to Biguhu Health Centre where he would get more attention from my brother while waiting for his departure.

My brother also convinced me that it would be better to take him back to Biguhu where he would try his best to take care of him until he dies. He discredited the medical care given to patients in huge hospitals like Kigali due to a big number of patients. He also convinced me that frequent visits from family members have positive impact on the patients' quick recovery. We therefore decided to take him back to Biguhu Health Centre.

Three days later, while in my office, I received a call from my brother that my father's condition was worsening. Our father was still in a coma from the time we departed and my brother was highly concerned that he had stayed too long in that critical condition. I quickly organized to go and see him again. This time, I went with my wife and two other Christian friends. When we arrived at Biguhu, my father was still in a deep coma. He was almost gone; the only sign of life was the slow heartbeat he had. We immediately engaged ourselves in an intense spiritual warfare, interceding for his healing. After almost thirty minutes in prayer, nothing visible had happened as he was still in coma.

Suddenly, Rose rushed toward my father; she gently laid her hand on his face and prayed a short prayer after which she stared at him without saying a single word. Suddenly, my father opened his eyes and greeted her. That was a big miracle because for many days, he was in a deep coma. We also rushed towards him and greeted him.

Immediately after greeting my father, Rose didn't want to miss that special opportunity of telling him about the Lord Jesus and His saving power. As she was talking to him, the rest of us continued with intense prayers on the other side of the room. After talking to him for a short while, Rose said: "Papa, you know it is a good thing to receive Jesus as your personal Saviour". She asked him whether he would like to receive Jesus at that very moment. My father replied that he would like to receive Jesus as his personal Saviour. He declared that he was ready to welcome Him into his life that very moment. Rose told him that to receive Jesus, one has to repent his sins and then welcome Him as Lord and Saviour of his life, acknowledging the accomplished work of Jesus on the Cross at Calvary. My father expressed his willingness to repent and welcoming Jesus in his heart. Immediately, as we were watching, my father repented all his sins before God. Rose led him through the sinner's prayer of repentance and my father received the Lord Jesus as his Saviour that very hour.

After making this greatest decision one can ever make while on earth, my father's face brightened. He was filled with exceptional joy and he was smiling. I talked to him and everyone had an opportunity to talk to him. The vision that Rose had, standing at the shores of Lake Tanganyika when she was a young girl was fulfilled in broad day light.

The conversation with our father did not last long. Shortly after, he fell again into coma. We again took more time in prayer. While praying, a prophetic message came through one brother. The content of the message was as follows: "This is the time to rejoice because what is pertaining to life is now in order; do not worry about the body". Some brethren interpreted the message as the guarantee that my father would get well soon but I personally got a completely different interpretation. I understood that my father got saved but would not survive the illness.

As we continued praying, another prophetic message came through the same brother. I thought the Lord had realized that many of us had not understood what He was telling us. The content of the new message was as follows: "Blessed are those who die today and are buried, because days are coming when people will die and have nobody to bury them".

To receive Jesus, one has to repent his sins and then welcome Him into one's life as Lord and Saviour.

We now understood that he would die but again, we couldn't understand what that message meant about people dying in the days to come who wouldn't have anyone to bury them. When we received this message, it was in 1993. God was talking about the Rwandan genocide that would take place the following year, but we didn't understand it.

What God said happened few months later in 1994. It was triggered by the assassination of two Hutu presidents, His Excellency Juvenal Habyarimana of Rwanda and his Burundian counterpart His Excellency Cyprien Ntaryamira. Also killed were top officials of both countries and the aircrew in the attack. Thousands of Tutsis were killed by *Interahamwe* militia who accused the Tutsi rebels of downing the presidential plane by missiles.

As the carnage over the Tutsis was taking place in the zone that was still under the control of the then interim Rwandan Government, thousands of Hutu civilians were also being killed by the Rwandan Patriotic Army (RPA). RPA had started killing Hutus in the areas occupied by the rebels. They later moved to other regions of the country. They finally conquered and gained control over the whole Rwandan territory.

Other thousands of Rwandan civilians were wiped out by RPA troops in Eastern Congo. Among those multitudes of Innocent Rwandans killed by other Rwandans, only the 'lucky' were buried. The rest were eaten by dogs; the beasts of the forest and the birds of the air, hence that prophecy we received at Biguhu came to pass.

Back to the issue of my father. We stayed for some time and then left Biguhu Health Centre for Gatare—the headquarters of CZN Project. This was a Friday evening. On Wednesday of the following week, in the morning hours, I received a call from my brother that my father had passed on. It was a grieving time for losing a loving father but at the same time, I was grateful to God that my father died after receiving the Lord Jesus Christ as his personal Saviour. I knew for sure that my father went to live with the Lord in heaven and hope to see him again when I finish my journey here on earth.

> Brothers and sisters, we do not want you to be uninformed about those who sleep in death, so that you do not grieve like the rest of mankind, who have no hope. For we believe that Jesus died and rose again, and so we believe that God will bring with Jesus those who have fallen asleep in him. According to the Lord's word, we tell you that we who are still alive, who are left until the coming of the Lord, will certainly not precede those who have fallen asleep. For the Lord himself will come down from heaven, with a loud command, with the voice of the archangel and with the trumpet call of God, and the dead in Christ will rise first. After that, we who are still alive and are left will be caught up together with them in the clouds to meet the Lord in the air. And so we will be with the Lord forever. Therefore encourage one another with these words.—1 Thessalonians 4:13-18.

Following my dad's death, I prayed that God gives me assurance that my dad made it to heaven. The Lord was so kind to me. In a dream, I saw my father in heaven. He was a happy man and looked much younger. I always rejoice whenever I remember that my father got saved as someone snatched from fire.

My father's funeral was attended by hundreds of mourners from different parts of the country, but as for me, there was no room for mourning in my heart. I was normal and charming. People didn't understand the reason behind that mien, but I explained later when I had the opportunity to give my speech. It was a favourable time to preach Christ who gave eternal life to my father few days before the end of his pilgrimage on earth. During my dad's funeral, many people gave their lives to Christ. A prayer cell started in the village and it was the beginning of a revival in my area. Some months later, my mother also gave her life to Jesus.

A Courageous Woman

The 1994 war in Rwanda was a horrifying experience. Many testimonies concerning the protecting power of God's hand towards my family will appear in a different book entitled, *"God's Protection During The Rwandan Genocide"*. For now, as far as the genocide is concerned, I only wish to talk about Rose's courage, this woman who was pregnant with twins during the darkest period in Rwandan history.

The account of events written in the following lines took place in the Nyungwe Natural Forest where we were hiding from massacres that were being perpetrated by soldiers of the new regime. In the forest, we were a group of 150 to 200 Christians (children included) hiding there. Every morning we used to meet together to give thanks to God for the new day.

It was becoming increasingly dangerous for men who were in some leadership positions of one kind or another. Being a Managing Director of an organization, I knew my life was in more danger. This made me not to come out to assemble for prayers.

One morning, as brethren assembled for prayer, somebody shouted with a loud voice, saying, "Silence everybody and hands up!" At this time, I was hiding at the opposite mountain. When the brethren looked around, to their great horror, they found themselves surrounded by armed soldiers of the Rwandan Patriotic Army (former rebels who had become government soldiers from the time when the new government was sworn in July 1994). The soldier who had shouted called two men from the group, one was a Methodist pastor, the other was an elder of a Pentecostal Church, to give the identity details of those in the forest and the reason behind their presence in that place. Those soldiers were calling the group a bunch of *Interahamwe* militia.

One morning, as brethren assembled for prayer, somebody shouted with a loud voice, saying, "Silence everybody and hands up!"

The two gentlemen explained that they were neither soldiers of the former regime nor *Interahamwe* militia but Christians who decided to come together with their wives and children for prayers because they had nowhere else to go. As the questioning of the two gentlemen was going on, some soldiers had already taken their combat positions, ready for action.

Another group of soldiers was busy searching if there were weapons in the small huts that were used as shelters. Instead of finding guns and munitions, they found Bibles, hymn books and food. Apparently, they were very hungry. They started eating the food found in the huts. A third group of soldiers was digging two large graves on the lower side of the mountain where bodies would be buried. When the brethren saw the soldiers digging graves, they were so terrified and understood that their terrestrial pilgrimage had come to an end. They sanctified themselves ready for departure heavenwards.

As brethren were being rounded up together (approximately 150 to 200 people, the majority being women and children) one young man sneaked quietly to escape. Unfortunately, before going far, he was spotted, captured and taken to the commanding officer who was to decide his fate. The commanding captain asked the captured young man where he was going. Trembling with fear, he told him that he was going to the next mountain to tell another lady to join the rest of the group. The young man was referring to Rose and our children who had not gone for the Morning Prayer meeting as Rose was getting more tired because of her pregnancy.

The commanding officer was surprised to hear that there were other people in the forest they had not seen. He left the surrounded group with his next in command, took six heavily armed soldiers with him and ordered the young man to lead them to the place where the woman he talked about was. From a distance, Rose saw the soldiers coming towards her hiding place. She quickly vacated the place and went hiding in the nearby dense bush. She took our three children (Blandina, Peter and Gloria) with her and instructed them to be absolutely silent.

Finally, the soldiers arrived on the site and realized that nobody was there. They turned toward the young man and started beating him mercilessly. While some soldiers were tying his arms behind his back, others were kicking him with their boots at the same time hurling insults at him and blaspheming the name of Jesus.

Rose was watching and listening to what was going on from the bush. When the beatings accompanied by too much blasphemy about Christianity and the name of Jesus intensified, Rose was moved by compassion for the boy. She said to herself, *if the young man dies while he was escaping to inform me of the danger, then even if I live, I would always have no peace in my life. Secondly, it is unacceptable for people to continue blaspheming the name of my Lord. I can't keep quiet.*

While struggling with these thoughts, Rose decided to pray speaking in tongues. The Holy Spirit spoke to her in a still voice and said: *Rose, do you remember? They overcame the devil by the word of their testimony and by the blood of the lamb.* This scripture brought peculiar strength and encouragement to her. She said to herself: *I am going to leave the bush and go towards the soldiers. If I perish then I perish but before being killed I will have told them the Good News of salvation and reconciliation with God through the Blood of Jesus Christ, and also requesting them to stop blasphemy.* She immediately jumped out of the bush and went towards the soldiers.

When the soldiers saw movements in the bush and a woman emerging, they lied down with their guns pointing at Rose, ready for action, but the Lord didn't allow the captain to give immediate firing order to his soldiers. As Rose was moving towards them, she was preaching to them in Swahili, telling them about Jesus and His saving power. She was speaking impetuously. She knew that she had to talk pretty fast, redeeming time, aware that the soldiers could be given order to open fire on her anytime. She was therefore trying to maximize the few seconds before any eventual action against her.

While speaking, Rose preferred using the Swahili language because, as the young man was being beaten, and blasphemies hurled at the name of Jesus and the Christian faith, the soldiers were also using Swahili and English languages. With a loud commanding voice, the captain ordered Rose to be quiet and to come over with hands lifted up. She kept quiet and moved toward them following the order of the captain. The first question addressed to her was, "Why are you speaking to us in Swahili?" "I am speaking in Swahili because it is my language," Rose replied. "How comes that Swahili is your language?" was the captain's next question. Rose replied, "It is my language because I am a Tanzanian". Wondering why a Tanzanian national should be in the Rwandan natural forest, the captain ordered her to produce identification papers to prove that she was a Tanzanian.

Rose, as a naturalized Rwandan citizen, was not in possession of any Tanzanian document, instead she presented her Rwandan passport that showed Tanzania as her place of birth. Her maiden name was also written in her Rwandan passport. When the captain saw Rose' maiden name, he remembered a certain Tanzanian official who was the Governor of Mwanza Province during a period he was a refugee in Tanzania. The captain asked Rose whether she was related to that man. "I am his younger sister", Rose replied. The seemingly shocked captain said, "Your brother was a good man, a wise man of great understanding. He was so kind to us during our time of exile in your country". The captain ordered his soldiers to stop torturing the young man and instructed them to untie him.

The conversation between the Captain and Rose continued:

Captain: Now, as a Tanzanian, why are you here and what are you doing in this forest?

Rose: Where else could I be? You are now controlling the whole country and you are killing people. As Christians, we decided to come here and have time to pray as we wait for what God has in store for us.

Captain: Who is your husband?

Rose: My husband is Celestin Mutabaruka.

Captain: Oh! So you are Mrs. Mutabaruka?

Rose:	Yes, I am
Captain:	We have now found you.
Rose:	Yes, you have found us; here we are. Did you wish to meet us?
Captain:	So, where is your husband?
Rose:	I don't know! Almost a month ago, he left me alone with our little children. He told me that he was going to Zaïre. As a pregnant woman, it was practically impossible for me to walk those long distances with other 3 young kids. He then decided to commit us into the hands of God and left.
Captain:	Why did your husband run away while everyone knows that he is a good man who was not involved in the killings that took place in the country?
Rose:	He decided to go because of reckless insecurity in the country. You are aware that many people, including those who were not in any leadership, are being killed. How much more for someone like him who was a director of an organization and you are aware that educated people are being rounded up.
Captain:	Madam, we are good people. We do not kill citizens.
Rose:	If you do not kill people and are not going to kill us, why are those soldiers of yours digging graves now?
Captain:	Madam, your brother was very good to us, therefore for his sake, leave the forest immediately. We have clear instructions to kill everyone we find in the forest and you can see that graves are being dug, ready to receive your corpses. Therefore, leave the forest immediately. We will report to the Colonel that we missed you guys. I am doing this at my own risk for the sake of your brother. You are now safe, quit the forest. Another thing I want to tell you, the God you told us about is really great. Today was your last day on earth. According to man's plan, you were to go to your God today but your God has overruled man's plan.

The captain instructed one of his soldiers to help Rose carry her stuff. He also informed the other commanding officer he left in charge of the larger group that there were some foreigners in the group. They decided to let everyone go. The whole group was instructed to vacate the forest at once. They were given fifteen minutes to implement the order. Everyone hurried to leave as fast as possible, leaving behind their few belongings they had taken to the forest. The two graves that were dug to receive their bodies were left empty. This was nothing but a divine intervention.

A Comforting Wife

From the time we left our house at Gatare, we passed through different hiding places. This time we were few kilometres away from Lake Kivu. I could see the mountains of Ijwi Island and admired them. I was longing to be there far away from the soldiers of the new Rwandan regime who were killing many Hutu civilians in different places in vengeance for the killings committed against the Tutsis.

To reach Ijwi Island was a big problem. More than that, I had mistaken it to be a safe place. Contrary to my thoughts, the Rwandan refugees who had managed to reach the island were insecure due to excessive infiltration of the Rwandan troops on the island. Killings of Rwandan civilians by Rwandan soldiers were taking place on this Zairian Island. In addition to the insecurity on the island, thousands of Rwandan Hutu civilians were dying due to hunger and contagious diseases such as cholera. This reminded me of what the Lord had told us earlier that there was no refuge in Zaïre. Sadly enough, when surrounded by clouds of problems, we tend to forget what God said and it pains His heart. It was utterly wrong for me to think of seeking refuge in Zaïre. Seeking refuge in Zaïre was contrary to God's previous warning.

While in that hiding place near Lake Kivu, my main concern was finding secure means for the exit of Rose and the children. The idea of travelling with them would put them at a much higher risk as men were the most targeted victims. My plan was to let them go first and then find my way out alone later. The plan was to send them to Zaïre, then proceed to the Zairian town of Uvira, where they would seek possibilities of crossing over to Tanzania.

One pastor, may God bless him, was organizing this for me, but at a later stage, Rose was not for the idea. She told me: "Celestin, I loved you and I still love you. I do not think that it is right for me to leave you alone and go to Tanzania. I must stay with you. If it means to be killed, then I am prepared to die with you. If our lives will be spared, then we will rejoice and give thanks to God together." These were sweet words to hear during difficult times but they were disturbing at the same time. The reason is that I wouldn't have wished to put her life and that of the kids in high risk. It would be better for me to be killed alone than the whole family.

One night Rose had a peculiar visitation of the Lord Jesus. While she was awake in the night, Jesus appeared clothed with glory. Rose narrated to me that when He appeared, she felt as if bones in her body were no longer joined together. She completely lost all strength. As she tried to lift her eyes to see the Lord's face, it was practically impossible. There were two reasons for this: One she had no sufficient strength to lift her head; secondly, the intensity of light that was radiating from the Lord was too strong. While struggling to lift her eyes, Rose managed to reach His knees. She couldn't see beyond the knees but at least she managed to see His glorious feet.

Despite the fact that Rose had lost all strength, she enjoyed peculiar peace in the presence of the Lord. Jesus called her by name and said: *Rose, do not worry about anything because I will protect you. I will even protect my soldier. Make sure that you are always with him wherever you go.* After some time, the Lord left and Rose immediately fell into a deep sleep. When she woke up in the morning, she told me everything about that glorious visitation, but she was wondering who the soldier that the Lord was referring to was.

I understood that the Lord was talking about me but wondered why He referred to me as a *soldier*, someone who has never been in the army. The Lord warned that we should never take different routes but stay together. Once again, we were strengthened by the Lord's assurance for divine protection. We never took different routes and the Lord fulfilled His promise of divine protection. Without passing through Zaïre, we left the country together. We give all glory and honour to God.

A Humble Lady But Rough to the Devil

As I explained earlier in the book, Rose is a humble woman. Nevertheless, this is not what the devil knows about her. She has been in the past and still is ruthless to him. She has inflicted severe damages into Satan's kingdom. Whenever the enemy tries to hit back, playing around with her children, husband and the Church of Christ, Rose arises like a lioness and challenges the devil.

Someone may probably think that I am exaggerating, but the devil and his demons know that they cannot stand their ground when Rose is electrified with the power of God, ready for battle.

The devil tried to have a go on our children

One time, the devil tried to have a go on our children using sicknesses. Rose was not amused. She went on her knees for two weeks without food praying for them. At the end of this time of prayer, victory was registered.

Another time, while I was at work, our teenage daughter Gloria suffered a sudden illness. Pain was so intense that the young girl was in absolute agony. Rose was at home with the girl. Rather than calling me to inform me that there was a serious problem at home, she did not want me to be troubled at work or interrupt what I was doing. She rather decided to pray asking God to heal our daughter. Instead of getting better, Gloria's situation grew from bad to worse.

Rose decided to change her prayer strategies. She asked the Lord to reveal the source of the trouble. Rose managed to get the hint from the Lord concerning the sudden illness. It was an attack from the enemy who was getting more frustrated as a result of the work Rose and I were doing for the Lord in the town of Ashford in the United Kingdom.

Following that revelation, Rose engaged the enemy in a fierce battle, commanding him to leave our daughter alone in Jesus name. After some time, the enemy left as he could no longer withstand the spiritual missiles that Rose was firing at him. When Rose sternly commanded the enemy to pack and leave immediately, Gloria shouted calling the mother saying "Mum I see strange beings running away through the window." God had opened Gloria's spiritual eyes to see the enemy leaving. Gloria was instantly and completely healed thenceforth.

When I came back from work, I found Gloria in the house, smiling as usual as if nothing had happened during the day. Rose told me the whole story of what had happened with Gloria and I was surprised but gave glory to God for what He had done.

A sudden attack to the husband

Another time, I also fell seriously ill. Mine was not as abrupt as Gloria's but rather progressive. I had terrible pain in the left side of my body from the shoulder downwards. After two or three days, pain in my shoulder ceased but more sharp and unbearable pain increased considerably in my left leg. It was as if my thigh was being ripped off by sharp knives. In fact, time came when I could not even stretch my leg. I would get some relief when I lay down with my left leg bent (my thigh and lower part of my leg forming an angle of approximately 45-60 degrees). Trying to straighten my left leg was terribly painful. We prayed and I also took some medicine but the situation was not improving in any way.

One night, as I was in agony, I decided to suffer silently so that I do not disturb Rose' sleep. She had spent the whole day at work and had come back home very exhausted. Although I hid my sufferings, God revealed everything to her. In a dream, she saw me struggling with unbearable pain and clearly saw something that was ripping my muscles apart. Still in her dream, she saw herself engaged in a spiritual warfare against what she saw ripping my muscles. Although her physical body was sleeping, her spirit was very much alert.

As I was awake, I could see her wrestling. Her body was in motion and she was speaking unclear words in a spiritual tongue. I knew she was dreaming. Suddenly, she woke up still speaking in tongues, left the bed and started walking to and fro in the bedroom praying. It was clearly visible that she was engaged in a fierce warfare. There was no more room for prayers in English or other earthly languages but battling with the enemy while speaking heavenly tongues unknown to the devil.

After a considerable time praying in tongues, she reached out for the bottle containing anointing oil; she put some on her hands. She removed the duvet from me and grabbed my thigh exactly where I had terrible pain. She said, "Enough is enough, I command you devil to leave my husband at once in the name of Jesus!" She then continued praying in tongues, still holding my thigh. Pain started moving downward from where she was holding towards the lower part of my leg. As pain was shifting downward, she was authoritatively commanding the enemy to vanish and her hand followed that pain's movement. With spiritual eyes, she was monitoring the movement of the enemy inside my leg. Suddenly, all the pain disappeared and I was completely healed. I stood up, straightened my leg without any pain, something that I couldn't have tried to do earlier on. I went to the toilet and came back in the room without any pain at all. From the second floor, I quickly went downstairs and came back upstairs running without pain. My health was completely restored.

> As the pain shifted downward, she was
> authoritatively commanding the enemy to vanish
> and her hand followed that pain's movement.

I joined hands with my wife and gave thanks to God for the instant healing. Rose told me the whole story, from dream to reality, and I was amazed at the working of the Lord. Having wrestled in prayer for a long time, Rose was clearly exhausted. For the remaining hours of the night, she slept like a baby. I also managed to sleep for the first time in that week and had a peaceful night. The enemy was completely defeated and he never came back again to torture me with the same sufferings.

The devil was ashamed during the service

This happened in Rwanda in the early nineties when Rose was living in the region of Crête Zaïre-Nil. Although Rose belonged to the Pentecostal Church of Rwanda, her ministry and the divine anointing operating in her life were accepted by many churches of different denominations in the country. Often times, they used to invite her for speaking in their services and conferences.

One day, a certain Methodist pastor invited Rose to speak in his church. That Sunday, the congregation was exceptionally big because senior officials of their denomination had visited the parish. In due time, Rose was welcomed to minister the Word of God. She started ministering under the anointing of the Holy Spirit. In the middle of her preaching, the powers of darkness suddenly became restless and started manifesting themselves. One woman who was demon possessed started screaming and the congregation was distracted from following the preaching. The church had never before seen such a demonic manifestation during the service. Everyone was scared and worried.

From the pulpit, Rose walked towards the woman. With the divine authority, she cast the demons out of the woman in the name of Jesus, commanding them to leave with immediate effect. The demons left the woman immediately and she obtained her complete deliverance from satanic oppression and she came back to her senses. People were stunned to see someone talking to demons and commanding them to leave and they obey. Many confessed that such miracles used to be performed by Jesus and His disciples as recorded in the gospels and the Book of Acts, but they didn't know that Christians today still have the authority to cast out demons out of people. That day many people believed in the Lord Jesus and there was great rejoicing in that church. The enemy who had purposed to distract people from receiving the message of salvation was ashamed and kicked out of the church. God confirmed His word with signs and wonders, and many people were born in the Kingdom of God.

Gifted With a Peculiar Forgiving Heart

It is one thing to talk about forgiveness, it is another to actually forgive. Practicing forgiveness is what God requires from us, not just talking about it. The same way He wants us to be doers of the Word and not just listeners (James 1:22), is also the same way He wants us to be doers and not just speakers of the Word. Our relationship and fellowship with God is complete when we *listen* to what He says; *say* what He says, and, finally, *do* what He says.

Below, we look at how Jesus emphasized the principle of forgiveness:

How many times to forgive?

Jesus taught His disciples about forgiveness. Crimes and other offences being common in the world, His disciples were interested to know from their Teacher how many times someone should forgive those who offended him. Jesus response clearly showed that forgiveness is a lifetime exercise and we have to forgive countless times. The following is the conversation that Jesus had with His disciples on this subject:

> Then Peter came to Jesus and asked, "Lord, how many times shall I forgive my brother or sister who sins against me? Up to seven times?" Jesus answered, "I tell you, not seven times, but seventy-seven times.
>
> "Therefore, the kingdom of heaven is like a king who wanted to settle accounts with his servants. As he began the settlement, a man who owed him ten thousand talents was brought to him. Since he was not able to pay, the master ordered that he and his wife and his children and all that he had be sold to repay the debt.
>
> "At this the servant fell on his knees before him. 'Be patient with me,' he begged, 'and I will pay back

everything.' The servant's master took pity on him, canceled the debt and let him go.

"But when that servant went out, he found one of his fellow servants who owed him a hundred silver coins. He grabbed him and began to choke him. 'Pay back what you owe me!' he demanded.

"His fellow servant fell to his knees and begged him, 'Be patient with me, and I will pay it back.'

"But he refused. Instead, he went off and had the man thrown into prison until he could pay the debt. When the other servants saw what had happened, they were outraged and went and told their master everything that had happened.

"Then the master called the servant in. 'You wicked servant,' he said, 'I canceled all that debt of yours because you begged me to. Shouldn't you have had mercy on your fellow servant just as I had on you?' In anger his master handed him over to the jailers to be tortured, until he should pay back all he owed.

"This is how my heavenly Father will treat each of you unless you forgive your brother or sister from your heart."—Matthew 18:21-35.

Forgiveness is compulsory for our forgiveness

To forgive is not optional but compulsory. The person who forgives benefits more than the one who has been forgiven. The following scripture is quite clear about it.

For if you forgive other people when they sin against you, your heavenly Father will also forgive you. But if you do not forgive others their sins, your Father will not forgive your sins.—Matthew 6:14-15.

Practicing forgiveness

I personally try to exercise forgiveness, but in some isolated cases, it has unnecessarily taken me many days to forgive because of the depth of the hurt. This is a weakness which I have requested the Lord to uproot out of my life and I thank Him because He is doing a great work in me. He has been helping me move from one level to the next in that area of forgiveness. For Rose, to forgive is not a big issue regardless of the depth of the pain. To my great shame, she is several miles away from me.

Rose forgives quickly. Regardless of the size of the pain inflicted on her, it is hard for her to go to bed with a grudge against somebody. She makes sure that she forgives the person who offended her before bedtime. I have lived with this woman for more than 25 years now; therefore, my testimony is based on a keen observation spanning a quarter of a century. Rose is always ready to forgive. I personally admire this incomparable gift operating in her life.

Some years back, Rose underwent very painful experiences. To make it worse, the people who were behind those painful episodes were not only Christians but also people in the ministry. My heart was so broken due to the harsh treatment that my wife suffered. God revealed my pain to one pastor. He sent him to come and pray for my healing. This pastor told me that God showed him a sharp arrow that pierced my heart and that arrow was shot by a brother of mine.

> God wants us to be doers of the
> Word and not just speakers of it.

Meanwhile, during my grieving time, Rose used to laugh at me wondering why I should allow my heart to suffer that much due to the devil's cunning schemes tailored to distract us in the ministry and other more important issues. She encouraged me not to bother about whatever she suffered, but rather thank God because it was such a precious training and a good opportunity for spiritual growth.

Due to the depth of the wounds inflicted on my wife, as her husband, it took me a long time to reach the stage of complete forgiveness and total healing, but I thank God because I finally managed to come out of that cage. I am now a free man. With Rose, her forgiveness was immediate and spontaneous, and this amazed me. The pain inflicted on her did not go beyond the period when those events took place. Whenever she remembers those episodes, she treats them as part of her history but they do not cause her pain anymore. Rose' forgiveness is not just for the outsiders alone, it is also for me. When people live together, chances are high that they may sin against one another or offend one another. And more often, it is more difficult forgiving people who are so close to you because their wrongdoing is mostly perceived as betrayal. But Rose is always quick to forgive me.

In our walk with the Lord, Christians have to reach a level whereby forgiving is straightforward, regardless of the size of the offence. I have learnt a lot in this area from this woman of God.

A Woman of Faith

Without faith, it is impossible to please God, the Bible says (Hebrews 6:11). Rose is a woman of faith. She applied faith in several circumstances and enjoyed the outcome. The following testimonies are edifying.

A swelling on the hand

A swelling developed on Rose' left hand in a strange way. Big and hard, it was like it just dropped there from nowhere. Surprisingly enough, it was not painful unless someone pressed it a bit hard. Though it was not painful, it was uncomfortable to have it. It had also deformed her hand. We prayed against it but it stayed for many months.

One day, Rose got annoyed with it and commanded the swelling to vanish in the name of Jesus. After that command, she decided not to pray about it anymore. Instead, she believed she had received her healing a result of which she purposed to continually give thanks to God for the healing.

The swelling still lingered but Rose refused to pray about it again but rather persisted in giving thanks to God for the miraculous healing. Rose was in for a 'patient faith.' The deformity stayed for a couple of months but one day, while she was in the kitchen, she realized that the swelling was no more. We rejoiced as a family to see what God had done.

From this woman of God, I have learnt that persistent symptoms do not necessarily mean that divine healing has not taken place. Medically, people are advised: *When the symptoms persist, see a doctor.* Spiritually, I would advise: *When the symptoms persist, engage a 'patient faith.'* Patient faith fortifies your resolve to wait upon the Lord; you will get your strength renewed (Is. 40:31).

What all this means is that it is important to believe without any shadow of doubt about the accomplished work of our Lord Jesus Christ on our behalf. Our physical eyes may see a different scene and our feelings may send wrong and discouraging signals, but what is important is to trust God, walk by faith and not by sight as we celebrate our healing gift. Surely he took up our infirmities and carried our sorrows (Isaiah 53:4a, NIV).

An eye duct blockage

It was one afternoon outside the Wye Anglican church, just after the wedding service of a friend. Something strange entered Rose' left eye. She quickly called me, requesting that I help remove what had entered her eye. She suspected that it was a small insect. It is a common thing for small insects to stray into people's eyes, especially when people are outside in the open fields. Strange enough, when I checked there was no insect or any other foreign object in her eye. The sudden discomfort had caused tears to flow from the affected eye. When I failed to see anything, we assumed that the insect hit her eye and left. We hoped that the pain and tears would be short-lived but this was not to be the case. The pain decreased but tears continued to flow.

As days went by, the flow of tears increased. We finally decided to make an appointment to see our family doctor. After medical consultation, the doctor said that there was a problem with Rose' eye duct. He prescribed some medicine and told Rose that if the problem persisted, she could see him again. Instead of improvement, Rose' eye condition grew from bad to worse. She booked another appointment with the doctor. After the second examination, the doctor realized that it was quite urgent for Rose to be transferred to an eye specialist at Canterbury Hospital.

The specialist at Canterbury did a thorough test and confirmed that the eye duct was blocked. The specialist tried to unblock the duct without success. After more sophisticated tests, the doctor reported that the duct was permanently blocked and told Rose that the only remaining possibility was for her to undergo an operation consisting of excision of the duct and then insertion of prosthesis. At that very moment, the Holy Spirit spoke to Rose using the scripture found in Paul's letter to the Corinthians that says: "Everything is permissible for me but not everything is beneficial" (1 Corinthians 6:12a). Following this divine revelation, Rose clearly understood that the choice was in her hands, either to undergo the operation as suggested by the doctor (permitted) or not, but it was neither compulsory nor beneficial. She rejoiced over the message and thanked God for it.

The doctor fixed an appointment for operation. From the hospital, Rose prayed earnestly asking God to heal her. She categorically rejected that sickness and started thanking God for healing. She decided that the excision of the eye duct and insertion of prosthesis were not necessary as these were not part of her divine inheritance. She adopted a strategy of waking up early in the morning (around 5am) to worship God and sing praises to Him with heartfelt thanksgiving for her healing among other prayer issues.

As time went by, the flow of tears increased. She was always in possession of a bunch of tissues for wiping tears. It appeared embarrassing because Rose was a secondary school teacher at the time. Standing before students in such a condition was disturbing but she didn't mind. Amazingly, as the flow continued to increase, she also increased worship and praises to God for her healing.

Almost three weeks later, one afternoon Isaiah our youngest son asked her what happened with tears as the flow had completely stopped. When Rose checked, there were no more tears and she did not even remember wiping tears that same day. She did not know the exact time when the healing took place. The problem was now over. It was such a marvelous time for rejoicing as a family to see Rose again without tears. This miracle edified us as a family and our faith made a considerable leap forward.

When Rose shared her healing testimony and the power of praise, the whole church burst into great rejoicing because everyone knew the problem she had been struggling with for many weeks. Her testimony was uplifting. That very moment, two women decided to trust God for their healing. One of them, the wife to the Assistant Pastor, had a back problem that harassed her for many years. She also started praising God from the bottom of her heart for her healing miracle. It didn't take long before that woman stood in front of the congregation, giving thanks to the Lord for her complete healing. She said that she was encouraged by Rose' testimony and realized that there was no reason to continue enduring pain while the Healer has already come.

Attack against a ministry co-worker

When the devil fails on one side, he tries on the other. He knows very well that he has no authority over believers but he schemes. He has always registered defeats whenever he tries to harm Rose, he therefore sometimes try to attack her co-workers in the ministry in order to discourage them and quench the fire of God burning in them. This scheme has not been working for him either. The following testimony is about Satan's assault on one of Rose' ministry co-worker while Rose and her team were on a mission abroad. The enemy purposed to kill and destroy but he again met a blatant defeat.

One time Rose was invited to minister in a women conference in a certain African country. She went with a team of six brethren. The rooms where they were accommodated had two single beds each. They decided to sleep in twos so that early in the morning all three teams may take time to pray in their respective rooms, interceding for the preaching and teaching of the day.

Rose shared a room with one sister. One night, after sharing the Word of God, Rose and her colleague went to their room. They didn't sleep immediately though they were lying on their beds. They stayed awake because they were sharing different testimonies. In the middle of their conversation, the other sister suddenly stopped talking and appeared to be struggling on her bed. Rose became concerned and decided to go towards the sister to see what was happening. Rose was shocked at the agony the sister was in. She had vomited a lot of blood. Rose couldn't understand what had happened with the sister. She wondered what to do that night as the sister continued vomiting blood.

It didn't take long for Rose to realize that it was an attack of the enemy who was determined to kill and destroy the sister and therefore cause great shame to the name of Jesus and to the ministry. She decided to pray in the Spirit and then take authority over satanic forces. After a short while in prayer, with a commanding voice, she said *"Devil, you are a liar and what you are trying to do will not bear fruit. In the name of Jesus, I command you to leave my sister alone now!"* She earnestly prayed for her, wrestling with the enemy and speaking in tongues. After sometime, the sister came back to her senses, and started talking.

Rose took her to the bathroom, washed her and cleaned her bed. The sister was completely healed. She testified that she had never had such a problem before in her life. It was a sudden attack from the enemy and this scheme also failed. When the assaulted sister came back from that mission, she was on fire for God. The Lord used her in a special way. She made herself available to be used by God in order to cause great harm to the kingdom of darkness. In fact, she was greatly used by God in different ways in that mission after her miraculous healing.

And after coming back from that mission abroad, the sister only spent one week with her family before she left again for another mission to Belgium. From this mission, she came back to the United Kingdom with an edifying report about the great works that the Lord did during her second mission. Many people were highly edified by the report.

Clean and Tidy Woman

Rose would feel uncomfortable to sit in a house which is not clean and tidy. Some women use having children as an excuse for not being clean and tidy in their homes. When we tell people, especially Westerners who are used to families with one or two children that we have five children, they do not understand how we manage to take care of such a family (cooking, cleaning the house and so forth). Whenever they come to our house, they always get surprised to find it clean and tidy, and this is not only in the living room and the kitchen where many people reach easily, but also in bedrooms and toilets.

Cleanliness and tidiness in the house do not happen automatically; there is rather hard work and tight discipline behind it. Rose has trained our children in these areas of tidiness and cleanliness. They are used to it. It is hard at the beginning but with tight supervision and consistency, the system becomes fully established in the life of the children and they start enjoying it rather than being a burden to them. Once Rose starts inspection on cleanliness, it does not stop on tidiness of rooms but also looks at clothes (especially underwears); teeth-cleaning after every meal; nail-cutting; taking shower daily; hair-combing; appropriate and respectable dressing code, especially with the girls. From time to time, our daughters get special hygiene and cleanliness sessions appropriate to the girls from their mother. I enjoy the clean environment in our house. Rose deserves more credits for this.

Rose and the Woman in Proverbs 31

The woman described in Proverbs 31 is an ideal woman, the dream of every man. The Bible puts it in a way that implies that she is not easy to find: *Who can find her?* the Bible asks. Of course nobody can find her on his own. She is a special favour that comes from God. Let us look at what Proverbs says about this woman:

> A wife of noble character who can find? She is worth
> far more than rubies.

Her husband has full confidence in her and lacks nothing of value. She brings him good, not harm, all the days of her life. She selects wool and flax and works with eager hands.

She is like the merchant ships, bringing her food from afar. She gets up while it is still night; she provides food for her family and portions for her female servants.

She considers a field and buys it; out of her earnings she plants a vineyard. She sets about her work vigorously; her arms are strong for her tasks. She sees that her trading is profitable, and her lamp does not go out at night. In her hand she holds the distaff and grasps the spindle with her fingers. She opens her arms to the poor and extends her hands to the needy.

When it snows, she has no fear for her household; for all of them are clothed in scarlet. She makes coverings for her bed; she is clothed in fine linen and purple.

Her husband is respected at the city gate, where he takes his seat among the elders of the land. She makes linen garments and sells them, and supplies the merchants with sashes. She is clothed with strength and dignity; she can laugh at the days to come.

She speaks with wisdom, and faithful instruction is on her tongue. She watches over the affairs of her household and does not eat the bread of idleness. Her children arise and call her blessed; her husband also, and he praises her:

"Many women do noble things, but you surpass them all."

> Charm is deceptive, and beauty is fleeting; but a woman who fears the Lord is to be praised. Honor her for all that her hands have done, and let her works bring her praise at the city gate.—Proverbs 31:10-31.

I wrote this book when Rose and I had been married for twenty-five years. I have had sufficient time to observe her and can boldly declare that by God's grace, I was exceptionally privileged to find this woman of such noble character. Rose is worth far more than rubies. I have full confidence in her and I surely lack nothing of value, thanks to her being hard working. She always brings good to me, not harm.

Rose is energetic and enjoys working with her hands. Her arms are strong for her tasks. She is like the merchant ships, bringing her food from afar. Rose wakes up much earlier than me. She gets up while it is still dark; making sure that food is ready for our children before going to their respective schools. She does many things in the morning.

Rose is a dedicated prayer warrior. The enemy knows that missiles would be fired into his camp if he tries to play games with her husband, children, brothers and sisters in Christ. Her lamp does not go out at night, she is always watchful. Even when she is asleep, her spirit is awake. In her hand, she holds the distaff and grasps the spindle with her fingers. Rose enjoys opening her arms to the poor and extends her hands to the needy.

During winter or when it is snowing, my wife has no fear for her household as everything is taken care of. The work of God and her family come first in whatever she does. People who know Rose say: *Blessed is the man who married this anointed woman of God.* I am respected at the city gate, where I take my seat among the elders of the land.

Rose is clothed with strength and dignity; she can laugh at the days to come. She speaks with wisdom, and faithful instruction is always on her tongue. She watches over the affairs of our household and does not eat the bread of idleness. Our children arise and call her blessed; I also do the same and I praise her from the bottom of my heart. Many women do noble things, but Rose surpasses them all. Charm is deceptive, and beauty is fleeting; but the woman who fears the Lord like Rose is to be praised. Yes, she is charming and beautiful on the outside, but even if this physical beauty finally gives way, her inner beauty will remain— it will never be threatened by the accumulation of years. I believe her reward in heaven will be great.

Money Management

Many families are set ablaze because of disagreement over money matters. Sadly, some of them end up splitting and living a divorced life. In such circumstances, children end up paying a heavy price over situations they are not responsible for.

In this area of finance management, it is amazing that since we got married, we have never had even a single argument related to money. We operate a joint account and we fully trust each other. Except for big projects which necessitate joint planning, otherwise each one of us can withdraw a reasonable amount of money without necessarily contacting each other. We thank God for mutual understanding and trust. As long as love is the foundation in the family, everything built on it succeeds.

Rose has no personal property; I do not have any either. Whatever we have belongs to both of us. We know nothing about management of individual private finances in our family and we do not seek to acquire such knowledge.

We are happy the way we are and we are satisfied indeed. Nevertheless, this does not mean that all people have to manage their finances as we do. It is not my intention to criticize husbands or wives who manage their finances independently. The mutual agreement on how to manage finances is what counts. If it works for them and does not affect their marital love and mutual trust in their home, they have nothing to worry about.

CHAPTER 8

A WOMAN WITH A BLESSED WOMB

~~~

"He will love you and bless you and increase your numbers. He will bless the fruit of your womb…"
(Deuteronomy 7:13).

Giving Birth to Special Children

So far, the Lord has blessed us with five children. They are all special and real blessing to our hearts. Blandina-Gratia is our first-born followed by Peter-Shalom. The third born is Gloria-Damaris followed by the twins, Deborah-Princess and Isaiah-Prince.

Rose holding a special 'card' for, "The Greatest Mum in the World" made for her by Deborah on a Mothers' Day (Deborah was approx. 6 years old then). According to her, the 'card' displays all the members of our family as follows (from left to right): Mum, Dad, Gloria, Isaiah, Blandina, Peter and Deborah. Such a wonderful card!

140

Blandina-Gratia Mutabaruka

Blandina-Gratia MUTABARUKA

Blandina, our first born, is full of grace. She loves the Lord Jesus with all her heart. She started preaching the Gospel when she was 3-4 years old.

At the age of 5, Blandina joined Gatare Nursery School (Kindergarten) in Musebeya Commune near the CZN Project head-quarters. When she was through with her kindergarten, she started her primary education in the same school.

The following are three of Blandina's testimonies concerning her heart for the lost. These happened when she was a young child, less than 10 years old.

Testimony 1: A challenge to the teacher

One Saturday afternoon, the director of CZN project organized a get-together for all members of staff as a way of appreciating their services for the project development. He provided food and drinks to everyone; all employees rejoiced. A disco was planned to last from evening till very late in the night.

Rose, being one of the members of staff, was present when the party began in the afternoon. Since all project employees were invited with their families, Rose had taken our two children along with her. I was not with the family at the time. I was in Kenya completing my master's studies. When the disco started, Rose decided to leave the place and go home with the children.

The following Monday, Blandina went to school. At the end of the school day, she went to her teacher and requested if it was possible to talk to her privately, where no one else was listening. Curious about what the little girl wanted to talk to her about in private, the teacher took her to a corner where other children could not hear their conversation. Innocently, Blandina told her that the previous Saturday when the disco started, she saw her drinking beer and dancing. She asked her teacher whether she was aware that God doesn't like to see people drinking beer and dancing in the discos in the night. Surprised at Blandina's observation, the teacher replied, "Thank you Blandina for telling me that, I will not do it again."

> Curious about what the little girl wanted to talk to her about in private, the teacher took her to a corner where other children could not hear their conversation.

The teacher didn't show anger to the child, but she was actually annoyed. We came to know about it later through other people. The teacher complained that Rose did not want to tell her directly that dancing in the disco and drinking alcohol were bad, instead she decided to send her little daughter with the message. This was the teacher's version of the story. Rose had not sent the child to talk to the teacher, it was Blandina's own initiative because at that early age she knew that getting drunk with alcoholic drinks and dancing in the discos were not godly practices.

Testimony 2: Leading someone to Christ and the healing miracle

At the age of seven, Blandina went to the house of one neighbour to play with other children. Her friends' father was away at work but the mother was in the house. Instead of concentrating on her friends, Blandina engaged Sophie (not her real name) in a conversation. Sophie was her friends' mother. Blandina shared with her about the love of God and how much He loves her. She went on to explain how Jesus gave His life for Sophie' redemption and invited her to accept Him as her Saviour.

Sophie had heard this message several times from different people before, but this time she was greatly convicted after hearing this 'same' message from a child. From that very moment, Sophie made the greatest decision one can ever make in life. She told Blandina that she has decided to accept Jesus as her personal Saviour from that moment. As Blandina was rejoicing for leading one soul to Christ, she laid her soft little hands on her shoulders and prayed for her. From that very day, Sophie became a Christian and started an exciting life with Christ.

Sophie's move to become a committed Christian did not please her husband who seriously warned her that she should forget about what he called "stupid beliefs". With humility before her husband, she requested him to let her continue with salvation, but the man was adamant, he rejected her plea. Although Sophie respected her husband, she found it difficult to abandon salvation. She was prepared to undergo persecution for the sake of Christ. When the husband realized that Sophie did not give up Christianity but was rather getting more committed to her new faith, he told her that she can go ahead with her daily prayers in the house but did not allow her to attend any Christian gathering either during the weekdays or on Sundays. Sophie's husband was a very strict man and Sophie was not free with him. She was always scared of him.

Sophie tried her best to comply to her husband's instructions but she was always torn between loyalty to her husband and loyalty to her Saviour. One day, contrary to her husband's instructions, Sophie attended the evening fellowship meeting with full knowledge that her husband was away and wouldn't be back until late in the night. That evening meeting was exciting and highly edifying. When Sophie went back home after the meeting, she was surprised to find her husband in the house. He was in the living room. The husband was fully aware from the children and the maid that the wife had gone to the Christian fellowship. Full of wrath, the husband had prepared a wooden stick, put it next to his chair waiting for the wife to come back home.

The environment was charged. Though they hadn't seen each other the whole day, there wasn't going to be any exchange of greetings. As soon as she entered the house, the husband angrily thundered with the first question, asking where she had been. Sophie chose to speak the truth but with sincere apologies. She humbly told her husband that she had gone for prayers. But in the middle of explaining and apologizing, her husband grabbed the wooden stick he had prepared and hit his wife on the back.

Sophie had a back problem that had been a real thorn in her flesh for many years. She had tried all she could to have her back healed but in vain—instead her condition worsened. Now as a result of an uncontrolled rage, her husband brutally hit Sophie exactly where she used to have more pain on her back. She fell down flat on the floor and remained there unconscious for a while. The husband became worried, his fury had been replaced with anxiety.

After some time, to the great relief of her husband, Sophie suddenly stood up. A miracle took place! At that very moment when her husband hit her back, the sharp physical pain that ensued replaced the diseased pain that had persisted. But the amazing thing was that when the physical pain inflicted by the husband subsided, the 'other pain' was also no more. It was the end of all back pains Sophie had endured for many years. God's ways of doing things are indeed beyond our understanding.

After the hitting incident, God miraculously touched Sophie's husband who finally allowed her to be attending all Christian meetings. When Sophie gave us the testimony about her experience, we were ambivalent. The fact that Sophie was completely healed was something to rejoice about. It caused laughter as an expression of joy for the healing; awe about God's ways; thanksgiving for her husband's change of heart; Sophie's freedom to attend all fellowship meetings, and prayers for her husband to be delivered from domestic violence and to receive the Lord Jesus as his personal Saviour too.

> At that very moment when her husband hit her back,
> the sharp physical pain that ensued replaced
> the diseased pain that had persisted.

Despite all these positive things, the mixed feelings were still justified on the basis that the violence that Sophie went through was chilling and dishonourable. It was obviously not the husband's intention to get his wife healed through beating, rather it was God's discretion to prove that all things work together for the good of those who love Him (Rom. 8:28). The humility and faith of an adult who responded to the Gospel through the mouth of a child was something so precious to God. He would not only honour it, He would also protect it in spectacular ways.

Testimony 3: The gift of faith in operation

A gift of faith operates in Blandina's life from her very young age. I remember one time when we went to Tanzania to visit the family relatives and found Aloys, one of her cousins, very ill. He was suffering from acute malaria. This young man was in his early twenties while Blandina was approximately 7-8 years old. As we were being welcomed and beverages served, Blandina was restless because of Aloys' pain. Moved by compassion, she went to the room where this young man was lying, fixed her eyes on him and she asked him how he was feeling. He replied that he was not feeling well because of illness. Blandina went ahead and asked him whether he was aware that Jesus could heal him that very moment. "Yes I know!" Aloys replied. Then Blandina offered to pray for him. She went forward, laid her little hands on her cousin and said a short prayer asking Jesus to heal him. She rebuked malaria and commanded it to go away from him in the Name of Jesus.

It was obviously not the husband's intention to get his wife healed through beating, rather it was God's discretion to prove that all things work together for the good of those who love Him.

At that very moment, a miracle happened. Aloys received his instant healing. He stood up full of energy and joyfully walked to the living room. Everyone was surprised to see him completely healed. Someone who was in agony few minutes earlier was smiling, full of joy and strength. When asked about what happened, Aloys replied that Blandina went in his room, laid her hands on him and prayed for his healing and the miracle happened immediately. Everyone gave glory to God for the way He used a child to display His healing power.

Peter-Shalom Mutabaruka

Peter-Shalom MUTABARUKA

Peter is also a young man of faith. From his very young age till now, his life is characterized by great faith. He trusts the Lord with all his heart. He does not believe in small things, but rather using his sharp eyes of faith to see great things ahead. Peter also has an extraordinary gift of giving.

Testimony 1: Receiving a bicycle by faith

Generally, young boys like bicycles, and Peter was not an exception. Between the age of 5 and 7 years, Peter had no bicycle and seriously wanted one. As I was abroad finalizing my studies for the degree of Master of Philosophy (MPhil), Peter approached his mother requesting her to buy a bicycle for him. Rose replied that she had no money to buy one for him, but she advised him to pray to God so that He could give him the bicycle. "Mum, why can't we pray to God now?" Peter asked. "Fine, let us go on our knees, close our eyes and pray", Rose replied. They both knelt down and Rose told him to pray for the bicycle.

After a short time of prayer, Peter lost concentration, opened his eyes and started moving from one place to another. He looked so scared. Rose asked him why he was worried and moving from one place to another instead of remaining in one place with eyes closed and concentrating in prayers. Peter's answer was mind blowing. He said, "Mum, I have already prayed and God has already heard our prayers and He is going to give me the bicycle. I have now decided to open my eyes and be watchful because God is about to release it from heaven; therefore I must have my eyes open so that the bicycle does not hit my head when it comes." The faith of a child! How do you 'kill' that faith by explaining that God doesn't give in that manner? The boy was ready to receive his bicycle.

Peter had unshakable faith that the bicycle was to come because he had spoken to the heavenly Father. To cut the story short, when I heard about the story, buying a bicycle for him became priority number one. The heavenly Father used the earthly father to get him a bicycle.

When he saw the bicycle, he was extremely happy and gave thanks to God for His provision.

Testimony 2: The gift of giving

Peter has a peculiar gift of giving. The following testimony happened when Peter was 12 years. One Sunday, we went to church in Eldoret, Kenya. Before the offering time, the pastor explained the meaning and principles of giving to God. He discouraged the bad habit of giving leftovers to God but give something of value. Since the offering for that Sunday was for the church building project, the pastor encouraged people to give a good offering or one of the things they like most, an offering that would touch God's heart.

That far, the church meetings were held in a tent. The pastor explained how precious it was to get the opportunity of participating in the building God's sanctuary. Peter was listening to the pastor carefully. People who had not come with their cheque books or money pledged whatever they wanted to give on a piece of paper and bring the pledged money or item the following Sunday.

What Peter did stunned us. He also wrote his pledge on a piece of paper without consulting us, the parents and took that piece of paper in the offering basket. When pledges were read out, we learnt that Peter Mutabaruka had pledged his treasured bicycle. He wouldn't let the opportunity to participate in the church building project pass him.

One or two weeks earlier, Rose and I had bought an expensive brand new bicycle for him to use for school. He liked that bicycle because over a long period of time, he had a dream of having that type of bicycle. After hearing the message concerning building the House of God, he decided to give his brand new bicycle to the Lord. It was not an easy decision to make as a young boy, but he did it. The amazed pastors of the church prayed a powerful prayer of undiluted and irreversible divine blessings over him. I have seen that prayer bearing fruits in Peter's life.

Testimony 3: The gift of wisdom

Beyond any shadow of doubt, the wisdom of God operates in Peter. One day, he said a word that I will not forget in my lifetime. We had joined a certain church in a country I will leave unnamed. We faced unbelievable opposition.

The anointing upon Rose' life was a big problem for Satan. This must have been the reason she became the main target. Rather than rejoice for the divine gift operating in Rose and be utilized for the benefit of the Body of Christ, it became a real source of insecurity to the pastor and his wife. When we realized that opposition against Rose was escalating, we had no other alternative but to leave that church following an advice of a wise man we considered as a father to us. We joined another church in the same town.

While reviewing the whole situation of the terrible circumstances my family went through and Rose in particular, Peter made an observation and said, "When we joined that church, the devil knew in advance that we would achieve a lot together and do more harm to his kingdom if we had remained united. He therefore tried whatever he could to separate us by bringing unnecessary strife and divisions. Therefore the problem was not physical but spiritual."

Gloria Damaris Mutabaruka

Gloria-Damaris MUTABARUKA

Gloria loves the Lord in an amazing way. We knew already that she is a special servant of God when she was still a baby. Even when she was still less than one year old, we used to take her with us into the prayer room. Several times, while praying for other issues, God used to show us Gloria in a vision wrapped in a special glorious white cloud. That she was a special child was also confirmed to us by different prophets at different times, prophesying marvellous things about her future.

As she grows up, God has been using Gloria on different occasions to convey special messages to the family. Her channels of communication with the Lord are clear and straightforward. Gloria is a person full of compassion. She loves people and delights in helping them in times of need. At home, Gloria is one of the most organized persons. At school, she is also praised by her teachers as one of the most hardworking students.

A singer

Gloria is exceptionally gifted in singing. Whenever she holds a microphone singing praises to God, she doesn't do it in order to entertain people but rather, to worship God with her sweet voice and the glory of God comes down.

In agreement with various prophetic messages concerning her future ministry, we believe as parents that through singing praises to the Most High under divine anointing, the Spirit of God will use Gloria to draw multitudes and usher them to Jesus.

A talented designer and entrepreneur

Gloria is a highly talented designer. You tell her to design something in her areas of interest, she will do it and the outcome is normally beyond the expectation of the person who requested the job to be done.

Beyond the designing capabilities, Gloria also has unequalled entrepreneurship abilities. Her financial and material prosperity are guaranteed if she continues to make God priority number one in her life and then work hard as she does today.

Deborah-Princess Mutabaruka

Deborah-Princess MUTABARUKA

Back in December 1989, God spoke to one of His servants to come and deliver a divine message that I am not prepared to share at this stage. "And this will be the sign that the message is from God," the messenger added, "Your wife will conceive and give birth to twins (a boy and a girl), call the boy, Isaiah and the girl, Deborah."

God is not a man that He should lie (Numbers 23:19, 1Samuel 15:29). On 23rd March 1995 (the sixth year from the time I received the message), Deborah and Isaiah were born.

A preacher of the Gospel

Like her sister Blandina, Deborah also started preaching the Gospel of the Lord Jesus when she was very young. Many times, from the age of 5 years, Deborah used pulpits of many churches such as Ashford Christian Fellowship (ACF), Wye International Christian Fellowship (WICF) and Fountain Church, among others, to preach the Gospel of the Lord Jesus Christ to multitudes.

During one of her sermons, she preached a powerful message on forgiveness. As a result, one couple that had started divorce procedures forgave each other and reconciled with tears of repentance. People gave thanks to God for the message and the miraculous reconciliation of that couple

A born leader and diplomat

There is no doubt to Deborah's gift of leadership—one can as well call her a 'born leader.' Wherever she goes, she leads. Madame Lamaison, one of Deborah's teachers at Lady Joanna Primary School made an interesting comment about her. She said: "According to the way I see Deborah, she will be another Kofi Annan to lead the United Nations".

During break time at Lady Joanna Primary School, Deborah used to organize other children and teach them. She even used to give them homework and surprisingly enough, other children used to obey and do them. They used to call her, "Teacher Deborah" and would follow her instructions to the letter. She also used to organize clubs at school and lead them. This was absolutely incredible at the age of 7—11 years.

At the age of 10, without our knowledge, Deborah approached the head teacher and presented him a project of starting a Christian Union in the school. Unfortunately, she was disappointed by the negative response from the head teacher. She then abandoned the idea of the Christian union but continued to witness to her peers one by one.

Deborah copes easily with anybody and gets used to any culture. When dealing with children, she talks like them, no wonder they like her so much. When talking to adults, she gives mature ideas that are well beyond her age. No one can be bored or fail to get something to laugh about when Deborah is around.

Isaiah-Prince Mutabaruka

Isaiah-Prince at the age of 10

Isaiah is a twin brother to Deborah. He is a boy of few words and a man of the Book. Isaiah loves the Bible. He has a peculiar interest in knowing what God says in His Word. He is always the first in the family to memorise biblical verses. He also likes quoting scriptures that match the prevailing circumstances. Just like his twin sister, Isaiah started preaching the Word of God from a very young age. At the pulpit, God has always used him to deliver powerful sermons that edify the body of Christ.

The value of promises

The following is one of Isaiah's most favourite scriptures:
"When you make a vow to God, do not delay in fulfilling it. He has no pleasure in fools; fulfill your vow. It is better not to vow than to make a vow and not fulfill it. Do not let your mouth lead you into sin. And do not protest to the temple messenger, 'My vow was a mistake'. Why should God be angry at what you say and destroy the work of your hand?—Ecclesiastes 5:4-6.

Isaiah hates breaking promises and vows. He expects everyone to go by his/her word. It looks very strange to him whenever someone breaks a promise. This quality already in him was strengthened when I once preached on the dangers of breaking promises. I remember Isaiah was the first in our family to memorize the above scripture when I also shared it with my family during our morning devotion. He does not understand why someone should break a promise or a vow. Anybody who breaks a vow or a promise would not have a fellowship with Isaiah. It pains him when a promise is broken.

One day, he was very tired and went to bed quite early. It must have been somewhere between 18:00 and 19:00. He requested me to wake him up after a couple of hours so that he may read his Bible. He had made a promise to God that he would be reading the Word of God every day, at least one chapter. When I went to wake him up some hours later, I found him in deep sleep and decided to leave him. Very early in the morning, he woke up and knocked at the door of our bedroom. Rose and I were still in bed. The boy was crying bitterly and we wondered what could have happened to him. When I asked him what the matter was, He said with sadness, "Dad why did you do this? I requested you to wake me up so that I could read my Bible and keep my promise but you didn't. Now look, I have fallen into sin of breaking the promise I made to God because of you. You did not do what I requested you to do for me".

I accepted the mistake and apologized to him. I then prayed with him and asked God to forgive me for not waking him up because I could see that he was very tired and deep in sleep after a busy school day. I put every responsibility on myself so that he could cool down. After comforting him, I also prayed for restoration of peace in his heart.

Isaiah is very keen with promises. From that time, he could never go to bed before reading his Bible as he promised God. Once Isaiah promises something, you can count on him. He also expects everyone to do the same. When we promise him something, we must make sure that we do it.

Unwavering personality for holiness

Isaiah, like his twin sister Deborah, is a young man with unwavering hunger for holiness. Once he decides not to defile himself with something, no one can make him change his mind.

One day, Halloween was being celebrated at his primary school. Deborah and Isaiah were 8 or 9 years old. They both refused to celebrate Halloween and partaking of the Halloween cake. Normally, Isaiah likes cakes but this time he was not even willing to taste it. When asked why he refused to eat the cake, Isaiah replied that as Christians they don't want to celebrate Halloween and eat its celebration cake because it is not a Christian practice or feast. The teachers told the two children that they were Christians too but they celebrate Halloween and eat the celebration cake. Nonetheless, Isaiah and Deborah categorically refused to eat the cake saying that they would not like to defile themselves.

The school rang our house to confirm whether our children should neither celebrate Halloween nor eat Halloween cake. Rose and I were not at home but our elder daughter Blandina who was 18 years old was in the house. She confirmed to the school that Deborah and Isaiah should not be involved in Halloween celebration. From that time on, it became known that the two children are committed Christians and the school was always careful not to involve them in any practice which would go against their faith.

A boy who believes in prayer

Isaiah believes in the power of prayer. I remember when he was eleven years old, he purposed to join Norton Knatchbull Grammar School for boys, one of the prestigious secondary schools in Ashford town. He therefore prepared himself for the entry exam known as "Eleven Plus". He revised past papers and we bought additional revision booklets containing more exercises from specialized shops such as WHS Smith.

One week before exam, Isaiah decided to take one day of fasting and prayer for his forthcoming exams. In due time, he sat for the "Eleven Plus" exam. He was quite excited at the end of the exam because he found that it was easy. He was sure that he did very well.

When the results came, he was not on the list of pupils who made it for grammar school. Isaiah could not understand what happened because he revised very well and prayed to God. He believes that every honest prayer has to be answered. I decided to appeal and his case went through. He was admitted to Norton Knatchbull Grammar School for boys. He was encouraged that his prayers and fastings were not in vain. He was pleased that God took note of it and answered him in His way.

Delights in praising God

Isaiah delights in praising God with drums and stringed instruments. The interest in drums was evident from a very young age. As we had no drums in the house, he used to arrange the cooking pots and dinning plates and beat them in the name of playing drums. Rose became concerned about her cooking pots and plates which Isaiah had changed into drum kits.

In order to encourage him with drumming at the same time rescuing the family utensils, we had no other alternative but to buy a set of drums and presented it to him as his birthday gift. He really rejoiced over this gift.

Using plates and cooking pots as drums was an important signal that the boy was highly interested in music, therefore we had to do something about it. For the guitar, he was given basic lessons by Kent Music School. He is now using his drum and guitar skills in the service of God. He is a member of Fountain Church Praise and Worship team.

Striker in his football team

Isaiah is a good footballer. He is one of the main strikers in his team. He scores many goals for his team. A couple of times, Isaiah appeared in the local newspapers for lifting high the banner of his team.

More family photographs

Blandina-Gratia at the age of 19

Blandina and the mother

Peter, Isaiah and their cousins in Brussels (Belgium)

Peter at the age of 17 with his sister Gloria

Gloria-Damaris MUTABARUKA

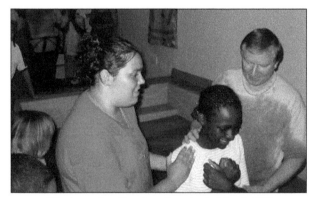

Gloria on her Baptism Day in Ashford, UK

Deborah playing in the snow

Deborah posing for a photograph with the snowman

Deborah and her twin brother Isaiah posing for a
photograph in the snow

Deborah-Princess at the age of 10

Deborah celebrating her 10th birthday anniversary with
her friends

Isaiah-Prince playing his guitar

Isaiah and team receiving game instructions from
their captain

Rose sharing a received text message
with Deborah

Family visit to Brussels (Belgium)

Deborah preaching the gospel in Ashford (UK)

CHAPTER 9
A HARDWORKING SCHOLAR

Academic pursuit has nothing to subtract from spiritual devotion. Blessed are they that allow their intellectual prowess point them to the One who gave the gift of knowledge. Is it any wonder therefore that "The fear of the LORD is the beginning of wisdom; all who follow his precepts have good understanding"? (Psalm 111:10).

Undergraduate Studies

*R*ose enjoys gaining more knowledge through education and training. Age and other commitments have not stood in her way. Her academic appetite is always unstoppable.

When we got married, Rose had a National Diploma in Forestry. While our first born was one year old, Rose was ready to start her undergraduate studies at Moi University in Kenya with me. Due to circumstances beyond our control, her desire was not fulfilled that year. Mr. Man (not his real name), someone senior in the Ministry of Agriculture, did not want Rose to go for further studies. He successfully managed to sabotage her scholarship arrangements. I learned from some people close to Mr. Man that he opposed Rose' scholarship because, according to him, it was not right for both the husband and the wife to have scholarships. The scholarship that Rose was to be given was a donation from a foreign organization. As Rose was obstructed from receiving that scholarship and no one else had applied for it, nobody was given that scholarship. That money was not used that year.

I was upset and angry at Mr. Man but I kept it to myself, but I was bleeding inside. I was so hurt I forgot the scripture in the Book of Romans that says: "And we know that God causes everything to work together for the good of those who love God and are called according to his purpose for them" (Romans 8:28, NLT). God however did not forget His word. He always watches over His word to perform it (Jeremiah 1:12).

As you will see later, it wasn't necessary for me to be angry at Mr. Man. When the enemy tries to sabotage our heritage, God would confirm his parentage over us, thereby establishing that no one can close the door that God has opened.

Because of what Mr. Man tried to do, God decided to make the arrangement even better for Rose. When I finally saw the outcome three years later, I had to repent before God for being short-sighted and for failing to understand His ways.

Our original plan was to start our studies at the same time in order to graduate together. This would ensure that we would avoid family separation over a long period of time. This did not work for us but Rose' ambition for further studies remained. It looked hard for Rose to get a scholarship as long as Mr. Man was in the same position of power. To solve the problem, we made a decision of selling everything we owned to secure enough money for self-sponsorship for the following academic year. This was our decision as human beings but God had better plans for us. If we knew, we could as well have appropriated Jeremiah 29:11:

> "... For I know the plans I have for you," declares the
> Lord, "plans to prosper you and not to harm you, plans
> to give you hope and a future..."

God had greater plans and blessings for us. Starting from the following academic year, Rose managed to get a full government scholarship award through Swiss Intercooperation, therefore we did not sell any of our property.

In August 1986, Rose joined me in Kenya at Moi University. Blandina, our first born, was 1 year and 8 months old and our newly born baby boy, Peter, was four months old. One month later, Rose enrolled for the first year of her undergraduate studies. At the same time, I also proceeded with my second year of study.

Studying while breastfeeding a baby and at the same time taking care of our first born who was also too young was not an easy thing to do, but Rose chose to face the challenge and overcame victoriously.

In 1989, she successfully completed her studies and graduated with a Second Class Bachelor's degree (B.Sc.) in Forestry. I believe this is a living testimony and a great source of inspiration to mothers who seek to further their education. All is possible and manageable to whoever is focused and determined to reach her goal in life. It is possible to bring up children and pursue academic excellence concurrently.

After her graduation, Rose went back to Rwanda with our two children and worked for the Ministry of Agriculture on a project called "Crête Zaire-Nil". This was an integrated rural development project that dealt with forestry, agricultural and livestock activities. Rose was in charge of research within the Forestry Department.

Postgraduate Studies (MPhil Programme)

In 1996, while breastfeeding the twins and having other three children to take care of, Rose embarked on a Master of Philosophy (MPhil) programme of studies in Forestry (Agroforestry) at Moi University. After her coursework on campus, she conducted research at the International Centre for Research in Agroforestry (ICRAF) at Machakos and Muguga, under the supervision of Professor Chin Ong[1] and Dr. Erick Koech[2].

Rose' research work was ranked, "First Class." Her thesis entitled, "Mycorrhizal association with *Melia volkensii* at Machakos, Kenya", was commended as a most excellent piece of work. Rose' performance was rated as a rare one (see letters written by the Head of Forestry Department to Professor Chin Ong and Professor Augustus Temu on the following two pages).

Another interesting aspect of her MPhil studies, was that Rose was the only student that far who completed within the shortest time possible. She used eighteen months instead of twenty four recommended by the University. A good number of students go even up to 3 or 4 years to get the Master of Philosophy Degree from Moi University. This is due to the intense research work involved in order to produce an acceptable thesis containing unique scientific findings. On the 4th December 1998, Rose graduated with a Master of Philosophy degree (MPhil) in Forestry.

---

[1] Professor Chin Ong is an expert in Agroforestry who worked for ICRAF for many years. Professor Ong is passionate about the potential of bamboo, a tree nicknamed the wonder plant which is the strongest and fastest growing woody plant on earth.

[2] Professor Dr Erick Koech, Forestry Expert and Head of Forestry Department at Moi University.

Rose's performance and the quality of her research was excellent and rated Grade "A"

Tel. Eldoret (0321) 43001-8/43620
Fax No. (0321) 43047
Telex No. MOIVARSITY 35047

MOI UNIVERSITY

P. O. Box 3900
Eldoret
KENYA

Ref. No.......................................

DEPARTMENT OF FORESTRY

23/09/98

Prof. Chin Ong,
I C R A F,
P.O. Box 30677,
NAIROBI.

Hallo Ong,

       RE: <u>ROSE MUTABARUKA - MYCORRHIZAL RESEARCH</u>

    Rose had a Viva on 22/9/98 and defended it successfully. Her performance and the quality of her research was excellent and rated graded "A".

    I would therefore Congratulate her, for the hardwork put into the research and congratulate you too for all the support you gave her to make the research what it has been.

    I suggest that you:

             (i)   Consider arranging for Rose to make a presentation at ICRAF concerning her research.

            (ii) assist her identify areas of thesis that are publishable.

    Thank you.

DR. E. K. KOECH,
<u>HEAD, DEPARTMENT OF FORESTRY.</u>

Rose's MPhil research was rated a rare one

MOI UNIVERSITY

Tel. Eldoret (0321) 43001-8(43620)
Fax No. (0321) 43047
Telex No. MOIVARSITY 35047

P. O. Box 3900
Eldoret
KENYA

Ref. No.............................

DEPARTMENT OF FORESTRY

28/09/98

Prof. Augustus Temu,
ICRAF,
P.O. Box 30677,
NAIROBI.

Dear Prof. Temu,

RE: ROSE MUTABARUKA

I wish to inform you that Rose had a Viva
yesterday and she performed very well. Rose attained
a grade A. The performance was rated a rare one
and indeed Rose deserves a "Congratulations note!"
I congratulate her and also thank ICRAF for allowing
her use ICRAF's facility at Machakos. I also
congratulate my co-supervisor Prof. Chin Ong for
advice given to her.

I now suggest that Rose give a brief presentation
at ICRAF, concerning her work soon!

Thank you.

DR. E. KOECH,
HEAD, DEPARTMENT OF FORESTRY.

Master of Philosophy Degree Certificate

MOI UNIVERSITY

Upon the recommendation of Senate
and on authority of the Council
hereby confers upon

Rose Mangula Matabaruka

the degree of

Master of Philosophy in Forestry

with all the rights and privileges
thereunto appertaining in witness whereof
we have hereunto affixed our signatures
and the seal of the University

on the ...... 4th ...... day of ...December............ 19 .98.

VICE-CHANCELLOR

SECRETARY TO SENATE   SECRETARY TO COUNCIL

Doctoral Studies

Life in England is not as easy as many people think. This is not just the case with foreigners alone, but also with indigenous Britons. Many people struggle for their living and the majority of the population is in debts. Many people who have not been in Europe, especially those who live in developing countries, have a wrong picture about the European continent. They think that Europe is a place of plenty where struggling for living is history. Let me tell them that the information they possess is not accurate and this should discourage economic refugees.

Irrespective of what level of education one possesses, it is not always easy to be employed in Europe. Many indigenous people with high academic qualifications are also unemployed. How worse it is for those from other continents! When we moved to the United Kingdom, my wife and I had Master of Philosophy Degrees. These are high academic qualifications possessed by few people.

We filled hundreds of application forms hunting for jobs that matched our qualifications. Many employers were not even bothering to acknowledge the receipt of our job applications. Only few were kind enough to reply saying, "Sorry your application has not been successful on this occasion but we will keep your details on our database".

As no employment was coming forth, Rose and I decided to maximize our academic potentiality in Britain—we would further our studies to doctoral level. We were encouraged by the fact that university fees for people with indefinite leave to remain in Britain were not as high as for people from outside the European continent. We applied for scholarships without success.

In 2000, Rose registered for a Doctoral Programme in Soil Microbiology at the prestigious Imperial College of the University of London (UK). She courageously embarked on this challenging programme of study without a scholarship. We worked very hard and managed to pay her fees for the first year. For the following years, God opened a door for her. An organization called Airey Neavy Trust accepted to pay her fees for the remaining years of her PhD programme. This was a big relief as she was not to care anymore about fees but raise money only for books and other items related to her studies. Fees were directly paid to the university.

Rose used to work with Residential Homes for
senior citizens in order to earn income for the family

The department celebrating Rose's successful completion of her PhD

Rose and her colleague with their supervisor Professor George Cadisch

For subsistence, we both used to work very hard during weekends and nights so that we maintain our family of seven. It was not easy for Rose to conduct a PhD research in Microbiology, an area that require more time in terms of laboratory work, and at the same time work with the Retirement Homes where she was to take care of senior citizens (old people), without forgetting our main responsibility of bringing up our five children. The whole mission sounded suicidal but Rose excelled in these three major activities (studies, work and bringing up children).

Rose' doctoral research involved intensive molecular techniques. She left no stone unturned to get command of her area of specialization. In spite of conducting this challenging research while at the same time carrying full load of family responsibilities as a mother and wife, Rose completed her doctoral studies with flying colours. Her research was rated as of high standard by Imperial College London.

During a colourful graduation ceremony that took place on 30th November 2004 at Albert Hall in London, Rose was conferred a Doctor of Philosophy (PhD) Degree by the University of London.

When the enemy tries to sabotage our heritage,
God would confirm his parentage over us, thereby
establishing that no one can close the door
that God has opened.

Rose's graduation ceremony on 30th November 2004 at
Royal Albert Hall, London (United Kingdom)

Doctor of Philosophy Degree Certificate

UNIVERSITY OF LONDON

Imperial College of Science, Technology and Medicine

Rose Mangula Mutabaruka

having completed the approved course of study and passed the
examinations has this day been admitted by Imperial College of
Science, Technology and Medicine to the University of London
Degree of

DOCTOR OF PHILOSOPHY

*Rector, Imperial College of Science,
Technology and Medicine*

Vice-Chancellor

30 November 2004

Rose (with a colorful jumper, seated on a wooden chair)
sharing a welcome meal with students. The event was organized by Imperial College Christian Fellowship, Wye Campus.

Research and Publications

As a result of her outstanding research, Rose managed to publish two theses and a good number of papers in well-known international journals. The following are some of her publications:

Mutabaruka, R., Hairiah, K. and Cadisch, G. (2006). Microbial degradation of hydrolysable and condensed tannin polyphenol-protein complexes in soils from under different land-use history (*Soil Biology and Biochemistry Journal, Vol. 39 issue 7 July, 2007. P. 1479-1492*).

Mutabaruka, R.M. (2004). Degradation of polyphenol-protein complexes by fungi in different tropical production systems. PhD Thesis, Imperial College London (University of London).

Mutabaruka, R., and G. Cadisch, (eds.) 2003. Regulation of N release from polyphenol-protein complexes by fungi in different tropical production systems, pp. 205-206. Wageningen Academic Publishers, Wageningen, The Netherlands.

Mutabaruka R; Mutabaruka C; Fernandez I. (2002). Diversity of arbuscular mycorrhizal fungi associated to tree species in semiarid areas of Machakos, Kenya. *Arid Land Research and Management 16(4):385-390.*

Mutabaruka, R.M. (1998). Mycorrhizal association with *Melia volkensii* at Machakos, Kenya. A thesis submitted in partial fulfillment for the requirements of the Degree of Masters of Philosophy in Forestry (Agroforestry), Moi University, Kenya.

Rose has also submitted a good number of manuscripts which are under consideration for publication. Some of those manuscripts are the following:

Mutabaruka, R., and G. Cadisch. Effect of polyphenol-protein complexes on soil microorganisms (Paper submitted to *Applied and Environmental Microbiology Journal*).

Mutabaruka, R., and G. Cadisch. Biological degradation of polyphenol complexes and nitrogen release by fungi (Paper submitted to: *Biogeochemistry Journal*).

Mutabaruka, R.M. and Kung'u J.B. Mycorrhizal and root modulation in some Kenyan indigenous trees (Submitted to *Forest Ecology and Managemenent Journal*, Amsterdam, The Netherlands).

Mutabaruka, R.M.; Mutabaruka, C. and Okalebo, J.R. The effect of *Leucaena leucocephala* alley cropping on vesicular arbuscular mycorrhizal population at Chepkoilel, Kenya. East Africa (Submitted to *Agricultural and Forestry Journal, Nairobi, Kenya*).

CHAPTER 10
DELIGHT IN APOSTOLIC WORK

"How beautiful on the mountains are the feet of those
who bring good news, who proclaim peace, who
bring good tidings, who proclaim salvation,
who say to Zion, 'Your God reigns!'"
(Isaiah 52:7).

An Inspired Zeal to Win Souls

ose is a typical evangelist but the apostolic ministry also operates in her. She delights in preaching the Good News of the Lord Jesus Christ so that people may hear the Good News of salvation. She also enjoys helping the new converts with teachings to ground and deepen their roots in Christ.

She rejoices in planting churches wherever she goes. The above characteristics have marked Rose' life from her youth until now. The zeal she has for serving God increases all the time. Through her ministry, God snatched many including her own husband from eternal damnation. Rose likes encouraging people. She cries with those who are afflicted and rejoices with those who rejoice. She intercedes for those in pain, those harassed and tormented by the enemy, and greatly rejoices at their deliverance.

From the time she accepted the Lord Jesus Christ as her personal Saviour at the age of 15 back in 1975, Rose has always been a pioneer and very active in serving God. As mentioned earlier, God used Rose to start a Christian fellowship when she was pursuing her secondary education in Iringa, Tanzania. From that time, the fire of God continued burning in her heart. Wherever she went: in schools, colleges and other institutions, Rose preached the Gospel of the Lord Jesus. Many people got saved and Christian fellowships were formed which were instrumental in strengthening the Christian faith in young believers.

At Rugambwa High School and in the National Service, Rose always lifted the name of the Lord on high. At Olmotonyi Forestry College, God used her in a tremendous way for the glory of His Holy Name. Many students acknowledged the Lord Jesus Christ as a result of her witnessing. This is the time I also made a commitment of giving my life to Jesus, welcoming Him in my heart as Lord and Saviour. Rose was such a great blessing to me as she helped me grow spiritually through intensive teachings and intercessory prayers.

As an instructor at Olmotonyi Forestry College, Rose continued to witness to students and members of staff. Many people repented their sins and acknowledged Jesus as Saviour.

Even after getting married to me, her zeal for the work of the Lord did not decline, if anything the zeal increased. She ministered in many churches in Rwanda regardless of their denominational differences. The Lord's favour was upon her, a result of which she was accepted by churches of different denominational affiliations. She never turned down any preaching invitation.

At Wisumo, the headquarters of Centre Forestier de Gisovu where I was the director of that project, Rose and I started a humble Christian fellowship which grew and attracted many people who gave their lives to Jesus. Today, some of those people are ordained pastors labouring in the Lord's vineyard.

From Wisumo, Rose went abroad to further her studies at Moi University in Kenya, as we had already seen above. While studying in this institution of higher learning, Rose continued with evangelism.

She evangelized students and members of staff alike. Hundreds of students became Christians. Moi University has a vibrant Christian fellowship which comprises more than a thousand born again and Spirit-filled students. Many members of staff also received the Lord Jesus as their personal Saviour.

Among students who received Jesus Christ as Lord and Saviour during one of Rose' preaching sessions was Daniel Owino Ogweno. The story of this young man is worth hearing. He has told his story in a book he entitled: *"Dreams of Hope and Visions of Divine Intervention: A Personal Story of an Eventful Life—This Far."* In this book, he describes, among other things, how God used Rose to snatch him out of darkness. From a sinner to a saint, God transformed Daniel into such a precious vessel into the hands of the Master.

Daniel Ogweno is a dedicated preacher of the Gospel of the Lord Jesus as well as author of life changing Christian books. Some of the titles of his books are the following:

- *VIRTUE THAT COUNTS: Pursuing that Which Touches the Heart of God* (Strategic Book Group).
- *A LIFE OF AN ENTHUSIASTIC WORSHIP: Secrets of Worshipping God in and out of Season* (Xulon Press).
- *LESSONS FROM THE ROAD: Understanding God's Ways Through Traffic Experiences* (Xulon Press).
- *THE SECRET WEAPON AGAINST TERRORISM: The Only Way of Capturing "The Most Wanted"* (Xulon Press).

After publishing his third book (*Lessons From the Road*), he sent a copy to Rose. When we opened the book, there was a hand written message on the first page. Daniel wrote:

Mom Rose,
Thanks for being obedient to God. The result is that you showed me the Saviour. May God bless you and anoint you that you may help as many as possible find their way to our eternal home.

Thanks!
Signature

Daniel, Skien, 18.09.2007.

As we continued going through the pages of the book, we came to page (v) and read "Dedication". The words contained in the Dedication message took Rose by surprise. Daniel wrote the following dedication message:

"This book is dedicated to Rose Mutabaruka, the woman of God who pointed me to the One who finally took my hand and said, "I am from There and I am going back There, come with Me! God brought you all the way from Rwanda to Kenya to point me to Christ. If you were to count a single accomplishment while you were studying in Kenya, make it this: That you were used by God to lead a soul to Christ!"

Rose was humbled to hear that God used her to point to Him someone who is currently blessing people with anointed books he has published and many more which are still in print. No one can remain the same after reading Daniel's books.

'Makeshift Church' Turned Prophetic

After Rose' graduation with a Bachelor's degree in Forestry from Moi University, Rose went back to Rwanda with our two children, Blandina and Peter. I remained in Kenya completing my two year programme for the Master of Philosophy degree. By the time she left, I had one year to go. On her arrival in Rwanda, she was employed by the Ministry of Agriculture in *Crête Zaïre Nil Project* (CZN). This was an integrated development project financed by the European Fund for Development (Fond Européen de Développement—FED). She was in charge of Agroforestry in this project.

Although she enjoyed her work as a forester, she was frustrated by the prevailing spiritual decay in the area. Her heart was burdened by the fact that people did not meet either in the week or on Sundays to worship God.

As the burden kept on increasing in her heart, she decided to organize the first Sunday service at CZN. This service marked the beginning of the regional spiritual transformation. That service was held in her house with a congregation of three people: Rose and our two children, Blandina and Peter who were 5 and 3½ years old respectively. Rose, the leader of that congregation, conducted the service for a period of 2 hours (the standard time for a Sunday service in Rwanda). There was a time for praise and worship, singing hymns and other songs unto the Most High.

Each member had the opportunity to give a testimony about the goodness of the Lord and what He is doing in his/her life. Rose preached the Word of God. Tithes and offerings were given as it is done in other churches. In brief, the service was conducted as if it was a big congregation. On the superficial look of things, it was like a makeshift church, more or less 'playing church,' but it was very important and highly prophetic for what was to happen in the near future.

Rose decided to organize the first Sunday service at CZN. Held in her house with a congregation of three people—Rose and our two children—this service marked the beginning of the regional spiritual transformation.

The following Sunday, the same congregation met again and conducted the service as the previous one. In the subsequent week, Rose started telling people about Jesus and invited them for the Sunday service at her house. One person responded to that call, to begin with. This means that during their third service, the congregation had increased from three to four. They had a wonderful service. Also the congregation agreed to have fellowship meetings for prayer and Bible study within the week.

Within few months, the group members increased in such a way that Rose' living room was no longer spacious enough to contain the congregation. She approached the project director requesting for a larger room within the Project Training Centre where members of the Christian fellowship would be meeting. As God's favour was upon her, the Director who was not a Christian responded positively and allowed Rose and her congregation to use the large room of the Training Centre for all their meetings, free of charge.

In November 1990, I joined the family at CZN after successful completion of my studies. Rose and I joined hands in the building of the Kingdom of God in that region. As many people continued to receive the Lord Jesus Christ as their personal Saviour, Satan, the enemy of God and of His family was irked. A strong opposition against the fellowship began. As Jesus was not opposed by pagans but rather by religious people who were claiming to be servants of God, the opposition against the work of God at CZN was not from declared pagans, but from religious leaders who were becoming more insecure and frustrated that some of their followers were receiving Jesus as Lord and Saviour.

It is ironic to see people who claim to be "servants of God" getting annoyed and upset by the new move of God. Instead of rejoicing that people were renouncing their evil ways and turning to God in reconciliation, the opposite happened.

Despite the opposition from malicious and envious religious leaders, the work of God prevailed and prospered. Many more people repented their sins and welcomed Jesus into their lives. As the room at the Training Centre was not large enough to accommodate the fast-growing congregation, we started the construction of the church building (a 28x12 metres' structure) using believers' contributions. The church was built with durable materials. Today, there are plans to expand the building to respond to the ever-growing congregation.

> Growth has the power and ability to
> turn 'small' into 'big'. Therefore, small is
> not a problem if growth is in the works.

To cut the long story short, as a result of the work of God initiated by Rose and our two children, today there is a dynamic evangelical church at Gatare CZN with many hundreds of born again believers.

By God's grace and for His glory, He enabled us to plant other churches in Muko and Musebeya districts, under the supervision of Gatare church. Two of them, Manji and Gashwati, both in Muko District grew up rapidly and later became independent parishes with their own pastors overseeing hundreds of members. I therefore take this opportunity to thank God for Rose because out of the vision and burden for the lost that He put in her heart, multitudes in Gikongoro province came to the knowledge of the saving power of the Lord Jesus Christ.

While doing her masters studies (1996-1998) at Moi University, Rose tirelessly served God in the Student's Christian Fellowship. Frequently, she also used to receive preaching invitations from different local churches. There was exceptional anointing upon her life as her sharing of the word used to bless many people. This explains why almost every Sunday was booked in her diary.

Relocation to the United Kingdom

At the end of 1998, our family moved to the United Kingdom. We spent one year in Oxfordshire then moved to Kent as Rose had to embark on her doctoral studies at Imperial College London (Wye Campus). Despite her tight academic load due to her highly demanding research, Rose could not miss time to witness to her colleagues and members of staff. She played a significant role in the University Christian Union. She is always remembered for her good work in that fellowship.

Following a revival that was taking place at Wye in general and among the student community in particular, Rose and I were requested by the leadership of our church to plant a new branch in the village of Wye. We prayed about it seeking God's guidance. Finally, we agreed to our pastor's idea and were prayed for as overseers for Wye congregation. It was a privilege to minister among the students community.

As the worldwide academic fame of Imperial College London attracts many students from all over the world, the main vision for Wye International Christian Fellowship (WICF) was to introduce those students to Jesus so that after their graduation, they would go back to their respective countries transformed by the saving power of the Lord Jesus, edified and discipled.

With the fire of salvation burning in their heart, they would be used by God to bless their nations with the Good News of the Lord Jesus, start Christian fellowships for the benefit of their own families, colleagues and communities. The Fellowship at Wye was such a great blessing to many international students.

After her doctoral studies, as she was busy applying for secular jobs that match her newly acquired qualification, the Lord spoke to her that He would like her to be full time in His vineyard so that she can continue being a blessing to His people through the anointing that He had placed upon her life. God increased a burden for the lost in Rose' heart.

She clearly received a message from the Lord concerning starting a Christian ministry, something that she was scared to start at the beginning because of the demands of the assignment and responsibility. God sent different messengers, including her own pastors that she has to move swiftly with the vision. Finally, Rose bowed to the will of God.

Friendship evangelism: Rose introducing Jesus to a
Peruvian woman

The Name, "Bells Of Revival Worldwide Ministries"

As already mentioned above, the divine instruction for starting a ministry had already been shared by the pastors of the local church and Rose had received their blessings. Nevertheless, she had no clue yet about the name of the Ministry. One day, as Rose and I were travelling from Oostende to Brussels, the Lord spoke about the mandate of the ministry that was about to start. The main mission was to ring bells to awaken the nations for a great revival. When we came back from Brussels, we paid a visit to our pastor at his home to share with him the revelation that we got on our way to Brussels.

After greeting each other, before sharing anything with him, the first thing the pastor shared with us was about Rose' ministry. We were surprised to hear from him saying that the time for ringing the bells of revival was due. We were surprised to hear the pastor mentioning *"Ringing the bells of revival"*.

The pastor asked why we looked surprised by what he said. We told him the whole story concerning the message we received on our way to Brussels. He was also amazed at God's coordination. This was a clear confirmation to us about the name of the Ministry *Bells of Revival Worldwide Ministries*. The pastor rejoiced with us and prayed for the task ahead of us as a family. This was quite encouraging. As preparations for the ministry were going on, we enjoyed the unconditional support from the pastor.

Finally, in 2008, "Bells of Revival Worldwide Ministries, BRWM" was officially launched and recognized by the United Kingdom.

The decision to start the ministry was not an easy one to make. After working hard to obtain her PhD in Microbiology from Imperial College London, Rose' dream was to be employed by international agencies or institutions of higher learning where we both had strong and reliable connections. Nevertheless, when the call of God became quite clear, she decided to drop everything and start a journey of living by faith.

Why a journey by faith? BRWM started without even a single penny in the bank account. She had to rely completely on God for the running of the ministry.

His Name is *Jehovah Jireh*

During her first two evangelistic missions, one to Plymouth (United Kingdom) and the other to Eldoret (Kenya, East Africa), the family did not have enough money on the account, but we agreed as a family that whatever we had should be used as a seed into this ministry for buying tickets for the servant of God. We trusted God that He would not let us go hungry in any way. It is nice and encouraging when the family speaks the same language of faith.

After buying the tickets, God miraculously brought back every single penny we spent. In fact, we received more money than what we gave as a seed into the ministry. God used different sources that we were not expecting.

As we all know, university students go through financial hardships. We were touched by their giving when they heard that "mama" was going on a preaching mission abroad. One student gave us a sealed envelope with our names on it and said that God told her to bless "Daddy and Mummy" with something little. As we were not expecting anything from this girl or any other student for that matter, we were not prepared to take the envelope but she really insisted wondering why we should block her blessings through the refusal of the gift. We finally but reluctantly accepted the gift. When we opened the envelope at home, we became speechless. The envelope contained two hundred British pounds. This was a big amount of money to be donated by a student.

Two days later, around noontime, someone came to our house and pushed something through the letter box and left. Rose and the children were in the living room. As this was not the time for the postman, they ignored the delivery assuming it was someone distributing business advertisement leaflets.

Some hours later, our daughter Gloria went near the door and collected the envelope which was a bit heavy. She gave it to her mother. When Rose opened it, she was surprised to find that the envelope was full of money. There was no note from the sender. Whether the money was brought by an angel or a human being, we have no clue till this day. After giving thanks to God, the next task was the counting operation. The envelope contained four hundred and fifty pounds.

This was not the end of God's supply. He also used many other people to donate for the mission and continued to support the ministry thereafter. The family got back what we had spent on the tickets. Rose also had enough for the evangelistic mission to Kenya.

God is faithful. When He calls, He also equips. He only waits for our "Yes" to His call so that He provides everything required for the fulfillment of His divine mission. The blessings of God to our family for accepting His call are much higher than material and attractive financial returns that Rose and I could have earned working for international organizations or other employers which could have been interested to hire our services.

Today, *Bells of Revival Worldwide Ministries* is a well-established ministry. One of its objectives is to establish a network of churches in Britain and other parts of the world. The first church "Fountain" has already been planted in the town of Ashford in UK. This church has been a blessing to many people. More than 80% of Ashford Fountain Church members received the Lord Jesus Christ as personal Saviour for the very first time in their life through the preaching of the uncompromising Word of God at this church.

A good number of couples that were on the brink of divorce applied the principle of forgiveness after being enlightened by Christ. For more information about Ashford Fountain Church, its website *www.fountain-church.net* may be useful. Some of Rose' preaching messages are on this Fountain Church website.

Also in fulfilling the mandate entrusted to her by God, Rose has been travelling to different countries of the world which include the United States of America, South Africa, Kenya, Tanzania, Uganda, Belgium, France, Sweden, Norway, Germany just to mention a few. As she preaches the Word and ministering to the people, God has always been faithful confirming the power of His Word through signs and wonders.

CHAPTER 11
CORRESPONDENCES

*I am writing to you, my beloved ones, to put words
to my feelings; talk the walk; express my gratitude;
highlight my wishes and point you to the values of
Christ, the hope of our destiny and the
Rock of our salvation.*

A Letter to My Wife

Dear Rose,

*I*n the Rwandan culture, it is not common for men to compliment their wives openly. In fact, there is a strange belief that
complimenting a wife is spoiling her. When a typical Rwandan man
from the village is happy with his wife, he would show it by actions
and never by speech. They know how to convey the message without
words. Surprisingly enough, the message is clearly understood and
appreciated by the recipient. For example, the man would buy special
and unexpected gifts to the wife, but he would rarely appreciate the
wife in words.

In a departure from and deliberate defiance to this culture, I want
to put words to my satisfaction because your life and deeds have

provoked me to do so. I owe you a verbal compliment. It would be wrong and unfair to fail to acknowledge publicly that you have been such a wonderful wife to me. I hope my testimony will not 'spoil' you. I love you, and so very much! You have proved to be a good wife and my closest friend.

I like the way you adorn yourself; not with expensive jewelry, but with goodness, godliness and humility. I can assure you that your inner beauty keeps on transforming your outward appearance day after day. You are beautiful and your beauty does not fade away. We are now married for more than 25 years but you look more beautiful than when we got married.

Your glowing physical beauty and flowing spiritual piety are gifts of rare blend—what more can a man ask for? You make me overflow with gratitude to God.

I pray that you keep on delighting yourself in the Lord, certainly a glittering crown is waiting for you in heaven. I am proud of you and I give all the glory and honour to God who, first and foremost, gave you to me and then made it possible for us to live together in love, enjoying rather than enduring our companionship.

God bless you indeed,
Your loving husband, Celestin.

A Letter to My Daughters

To my precious daughters:
Blandina, Gloria and Deborah,

*Y*ou are blessed to have Rose as your mother and to be brought up by this anointed woman of God. When you observe your mother, what do you see? She is a living example for you to follow.

Your mum's life has caused me, not only to write this book about her but also to sing. You are witnesses that your mum and I live a happy life. You have never seen us quarrelling or disagreeing on any issue. I wish you happy marriages and the good reports from your husbands will cause your mum and I to rejoice, making shouts of joy to the Lord.

We wish you to be good wives to your future husbands and trust God that our dream for you will come to pass.

I know your mum has more to tell you confidentially. Pay attention to her words of wisdom, treasure them and put them into practice. They will be like a precious ornament on your necks for a lifetime.

God bless you my daughters,
Your loving Dad

A Letter to My Sons-In-Law

To my precious sons-in-law,

I do not know you yet, but I have seen you already. Does it make sense to you? I neither know your names nor have I met you yet—probably I have, but I saw you coming, it is just a matter of time.

Your mother-in-law and I are convinced that you are the right ones for our daughters because we earnestly prayed that no disguised wolves in sheepskins should come closer to our daughters. I therefore welcome you from a distance and congratulate you because you are among the blessed of the Lord.

Although your both parents-in-law are doing a good job of bringing up good wives for you, what your mother-in-law is doing is tremendous. She goes into details for the benefits of your future homes with our daughters; fine details that I am unable to handle as a man. She deserves special honour from you.

When you see the cleanness of your future wives, do not think that it came automatically. It took your mother-in-law's efforts. When you see them as prayer warriors, do not assume that they were born that way. Every child, especially teenagers, enjoy sleeping in the mornings and weekends. Our children were no exception but as parents, we had to take a serious stand and the children had no choice but to comply with the rules of the house. In the process, prayers became part of them.

In your life with our daughters, make sure that God comes first before everything else. Together with them, make sure that you keep the fire of God burning in your homes. It is the fire of God that will keep your marriage warm and burn away any residues of the flesh that the evil one may want to manipulate. God's fire will also refine you.

Finally, I trust God that together with my daughters, you will do everything to bring up my grand-children in the proper way, especially in the fear of the Lord as this is the beginning of wisdom (Proverbs 1:7). This is one of God's expectations for marriage and parenthood. We read in Malachi 2:15:

Has not the Lord made them one? In flesh and spirit they are his. And why one? *Because he was seeking godly offspring.* So guard yourself in your spirit, and do not break faith with the wife of your youth (NIV 1984, italics, author's emphasis).

God bless you guys,
Your loving Father-in-law.

A Letter to My Sons

To my precious sons, Peter and Isaiah,

*Y*ou have witnessed how privileged I am to have your mother as my life companion. I am very proud of her. You witness how she trains your sisters to become good wives when they get married. Do you also pray for your future mothers-in-law so that they give appropriate training to your wives-to-be? Do you sincerely take time to pray for your future wives as well?

My sons, be careful in life. Do not be attracted by external beauty but rather seek the Lord before committing yourself to someone who is going to live with you for life, making sure that she is the right one. What matters first is the inner beauty than the external appearance. Do not make a mistake of marrying a wrong person lest you suffer for a lifetime.

Divorce should not be in your vocabulary. It is a disgraceful thing in the eyes of God. In fact, the Bible says in the Book of Malachi 2:16 that *God hates divorce.* Take sufficient time to pray to God for divine guidance in this delicate issue. Get confirmation and assurance from Him that the person you are going to get married to is the right one and then go ahead. I took time praying for a wife and God revealed your mother to me. I married the right person and now you are witnesses that I am a happy man.

When you get married, please make sure that you take care of my daughters-in-law. Make them happy. Be good priests of your homes and lead my daughters-in-law and my grandchildren in the ways of righteousness. Make a small heaven on earth and enjoy the real meaning of marriage.

God bless you my sons,
Your loving Dad.

A Letter to My Daughters In-Law

To my precious daughters in-law,

I am deliberately making a linguistic mistake calling you "daughters-in-law" before getting married to my sons. But even if this should face logical challenges, I will not shy from addressing you as such because I am persuaded at which dimension I am operating. If I see what has not come to pass, it is because of two things: i) It is the essence of faith—calling things that are not as if they are; ii) it is engaging the spirit of the prophet. A prophet sees in the former what is still in the future.

I do not know you yet but I know you are there. I already saw you coming into my family, beautifully adorned and shining from inside. Trust me, I saw you with the eyes of my inner man. Although it was like a reflection in a mirror, time is coming when I will see you face-to-face.

Based on what we believe for our sons, you are the right ones and your coming into our family will be a real blessing. Your parents-in-law know that you are the right ones because we prayed asking God to block the path of hypocrites who would attempt to marry our sons. We therefore express our sincere love to you and warmly welcome you into our family.

Your sisters and brothers-in-law as well as your husbands-to-be can't wait to see you face-to-face. In fact, once in a while, we talk about you and seriously pray for you. By the time I am writing this letter to you, you are not yet married to my sons, nevertheless know this in advance before joining my family: *a good wife is always rewarded*.

I hope that your goodness, gentleness, faithfulness, love for God and for your husbands will cause my sons to sing a song of thanksgiving to the Lord because of you. While testifying before people about you, I hope my sons will also use Chapter 31 of the Book of Proverbs to describe your character.

God bless you my daughters,
Your loving father-in-law.

CHAPTER 12

CONCLUSION

For the married couple: Life is full of challenges,
most of which the enemy deliberately put on your
course to make the journey difficult. There is enough
to keep you busy. Don't allow the enemy to add you
to the list of challenges that your partner
has to contend with.

"Houses and wealth are inherited from parents, but a prudent wife is from the Lord" (Proverbs 19:14). Besides salvation, there is nothing else more enjoyable than a good marriage. Even though one may pass through the valleys of the shadow of death, with a life companion who understands and who is always prepared to be with you until the end, the burden becomes lighter. With a wife who genuinely whispers words of love and encouragement to your ear, you can afford a smile in the midst of the wildest storm and tribulation.

When you are on a journey or a mission with full knowledge that someone is backing you with prayer and support, you can face any obstacle and tackle any challenges along the way.

To be with Rose has blessed my heart beyond expression. God answered my prayer and graciously accepted the criteria I submitted to Him when I was praying for a life companion. In fact, He gave me more than I asked because I found favour before Him as a result of my simple but genuine prayer. This reminded me of King Solomon when he prayed asking God to give him wisdom. He was yearning for a discerning heart to govern the people of God and to distinguish between right and wrong. The Lord was pleased that Solomon asked this and He said:

> Since you have asked for this and not for long life or wealth for yourself, nor have asked for the death of your enemies but for discernment in administering justice, I will do what you have asked. I will give you a wise and discerning heart, so that there will never have been anyone like you, nor will there ever be. Moreover, I will give you what you have not asked for—both wealth and honor—so that in your lifetime you will have no equal among kings.—1 Kings 3:11-13.

To refresh the reader's memory, my humble prayer to the Lord was, "A wife who truly loves the Lord with all her heart and who would be dedicated to serve Him all the days of her life".

The external appearance or levels of education were not among my priorities. I was prepared to marry an uneducated woman who does not know how to read or write as long as she was God's choice for me. God was pleased with the sincerity of my heart and gave me a wife who fully satisfied and even superseded the criteria I presented to Him. Rose loves the Lord with all her heart and she is committed and fully determined to serve God all the days of her life.

The same way God gave Solomon wisdom and other things that he had not asked for (riches and honour), God also gave me a godly wife who is also beautiful and learned. Rose is neither too tall nor short, her height is average. She has no body deformity; she is physically fit, energetic and hardworking. Even though I was prepared to marry an uneducated woman, God gave me one who managed to reach the top. As I have already shown above, Rose is a doctor. She was awarded a PhD Degree from one of the most prestigious institutions of higher learning in the world.

One thing I have learnt in all these things is that a honest and genuine prayer touches God's heart, consequently, God's response is beyond what we can think or imagine. His answer comes with more than we asked.

I sincerely thank God for this woman who has become part of me. She has always been a great source of joy and encouragement.

To God be glory, great things He hath done.

Thanks for reading.